# ADVENTURING

SENIOR AUTHORS

**Virginia A. Arnold**     **Carl B. Smith**

LITERATURE CONSULTANTS

Joan I. Glazer     Margaret H. Lippert

**Macmillan Publishing Company**
New York

**Collier Macmillan Publishers**
London

## ACKNOWLEDGMENTS

*The publisher gratefully acknowledges permission to reprint the following copyrighted material:*

"A Birthday for General Washington" is excerpted from A BIRTHDAY FOR GENERAL WASHINGTON by Johanna Johnston. Copyright © 1976 by Johanna Johnston. Reprinted by permission of Childrens Press.

"The Cabin Faced West" adapted from THE CABIN FACED WEST by Jean Fritz. Copyright © 1958 by Jean Fritz. Adaptation reprinted by permission of Coward-McCann.

"Can You Top This?" is an original trademark the concept of which was originated by Senator Edward H. Ford. Used by permission of the current registered owner. "Can You Top This?" contains excerpts from THE NONSENSE BOOK by Duncan Emrich. Copyright © 1970 by Duncan Emrich and from THE HODGEPODGE BOOK by Duncan Emrich. Copyright © 1972 by Duncan Emrich. Reprinted by permission of Scholastic Inc. Also from TOMFOOLERY: TRICKERY AND FOOLERY WITH WORDS collected by Alvin Schwartz (J.B. Lippincott). Copyright © 1973 by Alvin Schwartz. By permission of Harper & Row, Publishers, Inc. and Curtis Brown, Ltd.

"Chin Chiang and the Dragon's Dance" adapted from CHIN CHIANG AND THE DRAGON'S DANCE by Ian Wallace. Text and illustrations copyright © 1984 by Ian Wallace. (A Margaret K. McElderry Book). Reprinted with the permission of Atheneum Publishers and the author.

"The Code in the Mailbox" from "The Code in the Mailbox" by Kathy Kennedy Tapp, first appeared in *Cricket*, April 1984. Copyright © 1984 by Kathy Kennedy Tapp and used with her permission.

"Communication" is the text adapted from LET'S FIND OUT ABOUT COMMUNICATIONS by Valerie Pitt. Copyright © 1973 by Franklin Watts, Inc. Used by permission of the Publisher.

"The Conservation Club" adapted from THE CONVERSATION CLUB by Diane Stanley. Copyright © 1983 by Diane Stanley Vennema. By arrangement with Macmillan Publishing Company, a division of Macmillan, Inc.

This work is also published in individual volumes under the titles *One to Another* and *On the Move*, copyright © 1987 Macmillan Publishing Company, a division of Macmillan, Inc.

Macmillan Publishing Company
866 Third Avenue
New York, N.Y. 10022
Collier Macmillan Canada, Inc.

Printed in the United States of America.

ISBN 0-02-163530-7

9 8 7 6 5 4 3

# Contents

7

# One to Another

# Gila monsters meet you at the airport

Marjorie Weinman Sharmat    illustrated by Byron Barton

Think of a place you have never been to. What do you think it is like? What stories have you heard about it? Sometimes what you hear is not always true. The boy in this story has never been out West, but he has quite a few ideas about what life is like there. Read to find out if the information he has is correct.

I live at 165 East 95th Street, New York City, and I'm going to stay here forever.

My mother and father are moving. Out West. They say I have to go, too. They say I can't stay here forever.

Out West nobody plays baseball because they're too busy chasing buffaloes.

There's cactus everywhere you look, but if you don't look, you have to stand up just as soon as you sit down.

Out West it takes fifteen minutes just to say hello. Like this: H-O-W-W-W-D-Y, P-A-A-A-R-D-N-E-R.

Out West I'll look silly all the time. I'll have to wear chaps and spurs and a bandanna and a hat so big that nobody can find me underneath it. I'll have to ride a horse to school every day and I don't know how.

Out West everybody grows up to be a sheriff. I want to be a subway driver.

My best friend is Seymour. We like to eat salami sandwiches together.

Out West I probably won't have any friends, but if I do, they'll be named Tex or Slim. We'll eat chili and beans for breakfast, lunch, and dinner. I will miss Seymour and salami.

I'm on my way out West. It's cool in the airplane.

The desert is so hot you can collapse. The buzzards circle overhead, but no one rescues you because it's real life and not the movies.

There are clouds out the window; no buzzards yet. I'm looking at a map.

Before, whenever I looked at a map, I always knew my house was on the right. No more; now I'm going left, left. Out West.

Seymour says there are Gila monsters and horned toads out West, and I read it in a book so I know it's so. But Seymour says they meet you at the airport.

We're here. Out West.

I don't know what a Gila monster or horned toad looks like, but I don't think I see any at the airport.

I see a boy in a cowboy hat. He looks like Seymour, but I know his name is Tex.

"Hi," he says. "I'm moving East."

"Great!" I say.

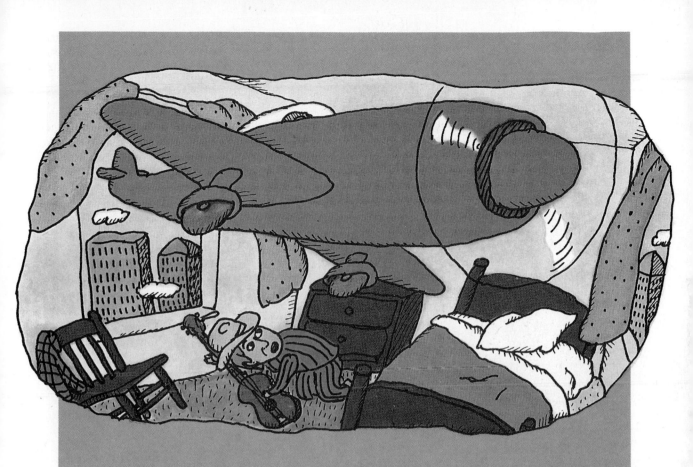

"*Great*?" he says. "What's so great about
it? In the East it snows and blows all the time,
except for five minutes when it's spring and
summer."

"You have to live on the 50th floor.
Airplanes fly through your bedroom, and
you've got to duck fast."

"They ran out of extra space in the East a
long time ago. It's so crowded people sit on
top of each other when they ride to work."

"Alligators live in the sewers. I read it in
a book so I know it's so."

Then the mother and father of the boy
who looks like Seymour, but isn't, grab his
hand, and he goes off.

"Sometimes the alligators get out," he yells
to me. "They wait for you at the airport."

It's warm, but there's a nice breeze. We're
in a taxi riding to our new house. I don't see
any horses yet. I don't see any buffalo
stampedes either.

I see a restaurant just like the one in my old neighborhood. I see some kids playing baseball. I see a horse. Hey, that's a great-looking horse! I'm going to ask my mother and father for one like it.

Finally we see our house. Some kids are riding their bikes in front of it. I hope one of them is named Slim.

Tomorrow I'm writing a long letter to Seymour. I'll tell him I'm sending it by pony express.

Seymour will believe me. Back East they don't know much about us Westerners.

## Questions

1. What two things did the boy in the story say he would miss about the East?

2. Did the boy at the airport want to move East? How do you know?

3. How do you think the boy in the story will like living out West?

4. Imagine you have a friend living in another part of the country. Write what life is like where you live.

## Applying Reading Skills
### Context Clues

Read the sentence below. Use context clues to choose the meaning of the underlined word. Then write the word and its meaning.

There's <u>cactus</u> growing everywhere you look, but if you don't look, you have to stand up just as soon as you sit down.

a. a plant with spines

b. a railroad car

c. an uncomfortable chair

d. a tree

# BIG TALK

Sometimes when someone doesn't quite tell the truth about something we say he or she exaggerates. To **exaggerate** means to make things seem bigger or more important than they really are.

Read each sentence. On your paper write the sentences that are exaggerations.

| In the West | In the East |
|---|---|
| People chase buffaloes all day. | Some people live on the fiftieth floor. |
| Cactus grows there. | Airplanes fly through your bedroom. |
| Everyone wears cowboy hats and rides horses. | It's cold every day of the year. |
| People eat chili and beans. | Everyone takes a taxi to school. |
| Gila monsters meet you at the airport. | |

Think about your home town. Write some exaggerations about life there. Here are some sentences to help you begin:

My town is so _____ that the _____. The people in my town are so _____ that they have to _____.

19

# THE GREAT MINU

Beth P. Wilson
Illustrated by Jerry Pinkney

The boy in "Gila Monsters" found out
firsthand what life was really like out West.
In this folk tale, a farmer leaves his village
and journeys to a big city. He expects life to
be more exciting in the city, but in his travels
he, too, comes to a new understanding. Read
to find out how a mix-up in communication
leads him to make an important discovery
about his own way of life.

Across the ocean and far away, a poor
African farmer got ready to make a journey.
He was going to the big city of Accra. He fed
his chickens and goats. He latched his hut.
Then he took off down the dusty road.

The farmer hummed happily to himself as
the morning sun came into view. How exciting
to be going to the big city! Nothing much
happened in his tiny village. But since Accra
was the largest city in Ghana, he would find
much excitement there.

Soon he reached the first village along the way. There he saw a woman on her knees, washing clothes in a stream of water. "Good day!" he called to the woman. "I'm on my way to the big city. I'm on my way to Accra!" The woman just smiled. She went on washing her clothes.

Farther down the road he saw some men and boys making iron. They were too busy to look up when he passed. But he called out just the same. "Good day! I'm on my way to the big city. I'm on my way to Accra!" The men and boys stopped for a minute and nodded. Then they went on working as if he hadn't spoken.

Soon he saw a grandmother telling stories to her little grandchildren. He loved a story and was tempted to stop. But he knew he must be on his way. He waved his hand high. He called out, "Good day! I'm on my way to the big city. I'm on my way to Accra!" The children turned to look. The grandmother smiled and waved. Then she went on telling her story.

At last he came to some farms just outside Accra. The first thing he noticed was a great herd of cows. He wondered who could own such a herd. Seeing a man with them, he asked, "To whom do these cows belong?"

The man did not know the language of the farmer, so he shrugged his shoulders. Then he said, "Minu," meaning, "I do not understand."

The farmer thought Minu must be a person. He exclaimed, "Mr. Minu must be very rich!"

Entering the city, the farmer saw some large new buildings in the town square. He wondered who might own the fine buildings. But the man he asked could not understand his question. So he just answered, "Minu."

"Good heavens!" cried the farmer. "What a rich man Mr. Minu must be. He owns all those cows and all these buildings, too!"

Soon he came to a great hotel with beautiful grounds. A group of African women came down the front steps. The farmer stepped up to them. He asked them who might own such a grand hotel.

The women smiled and said softly, "Minu."

"How wealthy Mr. Minu is!" exclaimed the farmer.

He wandered from one neighborhood to another. Seeing a large house, he stopped in surprise. "These homes in Accra are so grand. They are not a bit like the huts of my village," he said. Just then a woman came out. The farmer stepped up quickly and asked, "Please tell me who owns this fine house."

The young woman raised her shoulders. "Minu," she said.

"How silly of me to ask," the farmer said. "The Great Minu, of course." He stood for a minute, admiring the house and garden. Then he went on.

Finally he came to the harbor. There he saw men loading bananas onto a huge ship. The farmer asked a man, "To whom does this fine ship belong?"

"Minu," replied the puzzled man. He couldn't understand a word the farmer said.

"To the Great Minu also?" the farmer asked. "He is the richest man I ever heard of!"

Just as the farmer was setting out for home, he saw men carrying a coffin down the main street of Accra. A long line of people, all dressed in black, followed the men. People on the streets shook their heads slowly. The farmer asked one of them the name of the dead person. He got the usual answer, "Minu."

"Mr. Minu is dead?" cried the farmer. "Poor Mr. Minu! So he had to leave all his wealth. He left his herd of cows and his buildings. He had to leave his grand hotel and his fine ship, too. He had to die just like a poor person. Well, well, in the future I'll be happy to live a simple life. I will be happy to breathe the fresh air on my little farm. I will help the poor people in my little village."

The long dusty road back didn't seem as long as it had before. When the farmer arrived home, he unlatched the door of his hut. He looked around inside. Then he climbed into his own snug bed. There he dreamed of the good foo-foo he would eat the next day.

## Questions

1. What happened each time the farmer greeted people along the way to Accra?

2. Why did the farmer keep thinking that Minu was a person?

3. How did the farmer's trip to Accra change the way he felt about his own life?

4. Think about a trip you have taken. What did you discover while you were away? How did you feel when you returned home?

## Applying Reading Skills
### Recall Details

Think about "The Great Minu." Try to remember some of these important details about the story. Use complete sentences to answer these questions.

1. In what city and country did the story take place?

2. What was the farmer's dream when he returned to his village?

3. What does the word *Minu* mean?

# The Dog and the Deep Dark Woods

Dick Gackenbach

The farmer in "The Great Minu" learned something about life by traveling to a big city for the first time. Imagine seeing something for the first time. You don't know what it is, but you take a guess. Maybe it looks like something else you *do* know about. But things are not always what they seem. When the animals of the deep dark woods see things used by people for the first time, they have some funny ideas about what the objects are. Can a dog—who has seen the objects before—help them to understand the truth?

On a walk,
a long time ago,
through the deep
dark woods,
the wild animals
came upon
a man's boot.

"What is it?" they wanted to know. The animals had never seen a boot before.

"I know what it is," said the bear. "It's a plant! See here!" The bear showed the other animals the two strings that fell down the sides of the boot. "These are the roots, of course," she said.

"No doubt about it," agreed the fox. "Let's plant it in the sun," he suggested. "Perhaps it will bear fruit someday."

The bear, feeling very
wise, picked up the boot
and carried it along.

The animals continued their stroll through
the woods until they came upon a rusty kettle.

"What could this be?" they wondered,
sniffing the strange thing.

"We know," cried the birds, who did not
want to seem less wise than a bear. "It's some
kind of nest," they said.

"Look here!" said one bird, pecking at the
rim of the kettle. "This is where the bird goes in."

"And down here," chirped another bird
from deep inside, "is the hole where the eggs
are safe."

"Naturally," agreed the moose. "A perfect nest if I ever saw one."

Once again, the animals began to walk. The birds, flying overhead, carried the newfound nest by the handle.

In a little while, they came upon a cracked white plate. "Now, what is this?" the animals asked one another.

"It is the moon!" said the otter. "And it has fallen from the sky."

"What else could it be?" asked the rabbit. "It's round like the moon!"

"So it is," said the fox, "and white like the moon as well."

All the animals nodded. "It is the moon, no doubt about it!" they said.

Then, knowing they would need the moon when the sun went down, the otter picked up the plate and carried it along.

Soon, they caught the scent of another animal who lived in the deep dark woods. It was the dog.

"Look here, dog," the animals cried. "Look at all the things we've found."

"See!" said the bear with the boot. "We found a plant."

"And a nest," cried the birds with the kettle.

"And lucky for us," said the otter, "we found the moon, which had fallen from the sky."

Now the animals waited quietly for the dog to praise them.

"I hate to be the one to tell you this," the dog said, "but none of those things are what you think they are."

"Pooh! Pooh!" all the animals shouted back at the dog.

"You can pooh all you want," said the dog. "Some time ago I wandered far from the deep dark woods to a place where I saw many such things. That is not the moon," the dog told the otter. "That's something to eat from. It's called a plate!"

"That's nonsense," said the otter. "Who needs something to eat from?"

"Anyway, it's true," said the dog. "And that's not a nest," he said to the birds. "That is something to heat water in. It's called a kettle!"

"That's silly," said the birds. "Who would want their water hot?"

"And that," said the dog to the bear, "is not a plant. It's a man's boot!"

"A man?" said the bear. "I never heard of such a thing."

"Man and woman, too," the dog said. "They have two legs, and they can walk, and eat, and talk, like us. But they can do much more than we can."

"Hogwash!" huffed the bear. "How can man and woman, with only two legs, do more than I, who have four?"

"I admit they have no wings and only two feet," said the dog. "But believe me, man can make things like boots to wear on his feet."

The very thought of wearing anything on the feet made the animals burst into wild fits of laughter.

"Did you hear that?" roared the rabbit. "Oh, silly dog!"

The birds twittered and giggled. The otter laughed so much she got the hiccups. The bear held onto her big belly while the moose rolled over with tears of laughter pouring down his cheeks.

"It's the truth," shouted the dog. "Stop laughing or I will leave the woods forever."

"Go *(hiccup)* ahead!" said the otter. "You don't know the *(hiccup)* moon when you see it."

This made the animals laugh even more.

The dog was very proud and did not like being laughed at. "All right," he said, holding his head up high. "I will go and live with man. Perhaps I will be welcome there."

So, the dog moved in with man, where he was not only welcome, he was loved as well. He happily ate his meals from a plate and got rid of his fleas in baths of hot water heated in a kettle. And when no one was looking, he chewed on boots.

## Questions

1. What three things did the wild animals find?

2. Why didn't the wild animals know what the things really were?

3. Do you think the dog should have gone to live with man? Why or why not?

4. If you found something you had never seen before, what could you do to find out what it was?

## Applying Reading Skills
### Causes of an Event

Write reasons to explain why each of the following events took place.

1. The animals thought that the kettle was a bird's nest.

2. The animals thought that the cracked plate was the moon.

3. The dog said that man and woman could do more than the animals could.

# SKILLS activity

## HOMOPHONES

Some words sound the same, but they have different meanings and different spellings. You have to hear the whole sentence to know which word is being used. Word pairs like this are called **homophones**.

> Many people enjoy eating <u>chili</u>.
> In January, it is <u>chilly</u> every day.

The words <u>chili</u> and <u>chilly</u> sound alike, but they have different spellings and meanings. <u>Chili</u> and <u>chilly</u> are homophones.

**ACTIVITY**  Read the homophones in the box. Then read each sentence. Choose the word that makes the sentence correct. Write the whole sentence on your paper.

| wear | where |
|------|-------|

1. Animals do not _____ boots.
2. _____ is the subway?

| sent | scent |
|------|-------|

3. The dog could follow the man's _____.
4. Who _____ this letter?

40

| blue | blew |
|------|------|

5. The wind _____ through the cactus.
6. The cowboy wore a _____ bandanna.

| see | sea |
|-----|-----|

7. I can't _____ the game from here.
8. Let's take a walk by the _____.

| plain | plane |
|-------|-------|

9. The _____ flew over the river.
10. The book had a _____ cover.

| would | wood |
|-------|------|

11. _____ you like to see an alligator?
12. She put a piece of _____ on the fire.

| hour | our |
|------|-----|

13. _____ house is in the city.
14. It takes an _____ to drive there.

# Sam, Bangs & Moonshine

*Evaline Ness*

The animals of the deep dark woods didn't want to believe what was really true. Sam, the girl in this story, likes using her imagination better than looking at the truth. Make-believe can be a lot of fun. However, as Sam finds out, she must learn to tell the difference between real and make-believe.

On a small island, near a large harbor, there once lived a fisherman's little daughter (named Samantha, but always called Sam), who had the reckless habit of lying.

Sam said her mother was a mermaid, when everyone knew she was dead. Sam said she had a fierce lion at home, and a baby kangaroo. (Actually, what she *really* had was an old wise cat called Bangs.)

Sam even said that Bangs could talk if and when he wanted to.

Sam said this. Sam said that. But whatever Sam said you could never believe. Even Bangs yawned and shook his head when she said the ragged old rug on the doorstep was a chariot drawn by dragons.

Early one morning, before Sam's father left in his fishing boat to be gone all day, he hugged Sam hard and said, "Today, for a change, talk REAL not MOONSHINE. MOONSHINE spells trouble."

Sam promised. But while she washed the dishes, made the beds, and swept the floor, she wondered what he meant. When she asked Bangs to explain REAL and MOONSHINE, Bangs jumped on her shoulder and purred, "MOONSHINE is flummadiddle. REAL is the opposite."

Sam decided that Bangs made no sense whatever.

When the sun made a golden star on the cracked window, Sam knew it was time to expect Thomas.

At the same time every day Thomas rode to Sam's house and begged to see her baby kangaroo. You see, Thomas really believed Sam.

Every day Sam told Thomas it had just "stepped out." She sent Thomas everywhere to find it. She sent him to the tallest trees where, she said, it was visiting owls. Or perhaps it was up in the old windmill, grinding corn for its evening meal.

"It might be," said Sam, "in the lighthouse tower, warning ships at sea."

"Or maybe," she said, "it's asleep on the sand. Somewhere, anywhere on the beach."

Wherever Sam sent Thomas, he went. He climbed up trees, ran down steps, and scoured the beach, but he never found Sam's baby kangaroo.

While Thomas searched, Sam sat in her chariot and was drawn by dragons to faraway secret worlds.

Today
when Thomas
arrived, Sam said,
"That baby kangaroo
just left to visit my mermaid
mother in a cave behind Blue Rock."

Sam watched Thomas race away on his
bicycle over the narrow stretch that led to
Blue Rock. Then she sat down in her chariot.
Bangs came out of the house and sat down
beside Sam. With his head turned in the
direction of Thomas, Bangs said, "When the
tide comes up, it covers the road to Blue Rock.
Tide rises early today."

46

Sam looked at Bangs for a
minute. Then she said, "Pardon
me while I go to the moon."

Bangs stood up. He stretched
his front legs. Then he stretched
his back legs. Slowly he stalked
away from Sam toward Blue Rock.

Sam was so busy thinking that she was
unaware of thick muddy clouds that blocked
out the sun. Nor did she hear the rumble of
thunder. She was almost knocked off the
doorstep by a sudden gust of wind.

Sam leaped into the house and slammed
the door. She went to the window to look at
Blue Rock, but she could see nothing through
the grey ribbed curtain of rain. She wondered
where Thomas was. She wondered where
Bangs was. Sam stood there looking at
nothing, trying to swallow the lump that rose
in her throat.

Sam was still at the window when her father burst into the house. Water streamed from his hat and oozed from his boots. Sam ran to him screaming, "Bangs and Thomas are out on the rock! Blue Rock! Bangs and Thomas!"

As her father turned quickly and ran out the door, he ordered Sam to stay in the house. "And pray that the tide hasn't covered the rock!" he yelled.

When her father had gone, Sam sat down. She listened to the rain hammer on the tin roof. Then suddenly it stopped. Sam closed her eyes and mouth, tight. She waited in the quiet room. It seemed to her that she waited forever.

At last she heard her father's footsteps outside. She flung open the door and said one word: "Bangs?"

Sam's father shook his head. "He was washed away," he said. "But I found Thomas on the rock. I brought him back in the boat. He's home now, safe in bed. Can you tell me how all this happened?"

Sam started to explain, but sobs choked her. She cried so hard that it was a long time before her father understood everything.

Finally, Sam's father said, "Go to bed now. But before you go to sleep, Sam, tell yourself the difference between REAL and MOONSHINE."

Sam went to her room and crept into bed. With her eyes wide open she thought about REAL and MOONSHINE.

MOONSHINE was a mermaid mother, a fierce lion, a chariot drawn by dragons, and certainly a baby kangaroo. It was all flummadiddle just as Bangs had told her. Or *had* he told her? Wouldn't her father say that a cat's talking was MOONSHINE?

REAL was no mother at all. REAL was her father and Bangs, and now there wasn't even Bangs. Tears welled up in Sam's eyes again. They ran down into her ears making a scratching noise. Sam sat up. The scratching was not in her ears. It was at the window. As Sam stared, two enormous yellow eyes appeared and stared back. Sam sprang from her bed and opened the window. There sat Bangs.

"Oh, Bangs!" cried Sam, as she grabbed and smothered him with kisses. "What happened to you?"

Bangs told her that one moment he was on the rock with Thomas and the next he was lying at the foot of the lighthouse tower a mile away. All done by waves.

Sam patted Bangs. "Well, at least it's not flummadiddle. . . ." Sam paused. She looked up to see her father standing in the doorway.

"Look! Bangs is home!" shouted Sam.

"Hello, Bangs. What's not flummadiddle?" asked Sam's father.

"Bangs! And you! And Thomas!" answered
Sam. "Oh, Daddy! I'll always know the
difference between REAL and MOONSHINE
now. Bangs and Thomas were almost lost
because of MOONSHINE. Bangs told me."

"He *told* you?" questioned Sam's father.

"Well, he would have *if* he could talk,"
said Sam. Then she added sadly, "I know cats
can't talk like people, but I almost believed I
*did* have a kangaroo."

"There's good MOONSHINE and bad
MOONSHINE," her father said. "The important
thing is to know the difference." He kissed
Sam good night and left the room.

## Questions

1. Where did Sam say the baby kangaroo was when Thomas came to see it?

2. What happened to Thomas and Bangs on Blue Rock?

3. Do you think Sam *really* learned the difference between REAL and MOONSHINE? Explain your answer.

4. Give an example of good MOONSHINE and an example of bad MOONSHINE.

## Applying Reading Skills
### Realism and Fantasy

Write these headings on your paper:

*Could Happen*   *Could Only Happen in a Fantasy*

Then write each of the following sentences under the proper heading.

Sam lived on a small island, near a large harbor.

Bangs could talk if and when he wanted.

Sam had a lion and a kangaroo as pets.

The sun made a golden star on the cracked window.

Sam was almost knocked off the doorstep by a sudden gust of wind.

# I DREAM A DREAM

I dream a dream by day
  a wish, a hope
  a fitful fantasy
  in which what isn't is,
  and where what is
  has changed
  or gone away.

I dream a dream by night
  a distant trek
  a journey through moonlight,
  and then what was seems dear,
  and waking find
  that all that is
  is right.

Felice Holman

# Why Mosquitoes Buzz In People's Ears

Verna Aardema                    Illustrated by  Leo and Diane Dillon

**Sam learned the difference between REAL and MOONSHINE, but it wasn't easy. It is often hard to understand the truth about something. This folk tale is a special kind of story that tells why something is the way it is. It is a "why" story. When you read this tale, you will learn why some people believe mosquitoes buzz in people's ears.**

One morning a mosquito saw an iguana drinking at a waterhole. The mosquito said, "Iguana, you will never believe what I saw yesterday."

"Try me," said the iguana.

The mosquito said, "I saw a farmer digging yams that were almost as big as I am."

"What's a mosquito compared to a yam?" snapped the iguana. "I would rather not listen to such nonsense!" Then he stuck two sticks in his ears and went off, mek, mek, mek, mek, through the reeds.

The iguana was still grumbling to himself when he happened to pass by a python. The big snake raised his head and said, "Good morning, Iguana." The iguana did not answer but lumbered on, bobbing his head, badamin, badamin.

"Now, why won't he speak to me?" said the python to himself. "Iguana must be angry about something. I'm afraid he is plotting some mischief against me!" He began looking for somewhere to hide. The first likely place he found was a rabbit hole, and in it he went, wasawusu, wasawusu, wasawusu.

When the rabbit saw the big snake coming, she was terrified. She ran out through her back way and bounded, krik, krik, krik, across a clearing.

A crow saw the rabbit running for her
life. He flew into the forest crying kaa, kaa,
kaa! It was his duty to spread the alarm in
case of danger.

A monkey heard the crow. He was sure
that some dangerous beast was near. He began
screeching and leaping kili wili through the
trees to warn the other animals.

As the monkey was crashing through the
treetops, he happened to land on a dead
branch. It broke and fell on an owl's nest,
killing one of the owlets.

Mother Owl was not at home. For though she usually hunted only at night, this morning she was still out searching for food to satisfy her hungry babies. When she returned to the nest, she found one of them dead. Her other children told her that the monkey had killed it. All that day and all that night, she sat in her tree—so sad, so sad, so sad!

Now it was Mother Owl who woke the sun each day so that the dawn could come. But this time, when she should have hooted for the sun, she did not do it.

The night grew longer and longer. The animals of the forest knew it was lasting much too long. They feared that the sun would never come back.

At last King Lion called a meeting of the
animals. They came and sat down, pem, pem,
pem, around a council fire. Mother Owl did
not come, so the antelope was sent to fetch
her.

When she arrived, King Lion asked,
"Mother Owl, why have you not called the
sun? The night has lasted long, long, long,
and everyone is worried."

Mother Owl said, "Monkey killed one of
my owlets. Because of that, I cannot bear to
wake the sun."

The king said to the gathered animals:
"Did you hear? It was the monkey who killed
the owlet—and now Mother Owl won't wake
the sun so that the day can come."

Then King Lion called the monkey. "Monkey," said the king, "why did you kill one of Mother Owl's babies?"

"Oh, King," said the monkey, "it was the crow's fault. He was calling and calling to warn us of danger. I went leaping through the trees to help. A branch broke, and it fell taaa on the owl's nest."

The king said to the council: "So, it was the crow who alarmed the monkey, who killed the owlet—and now Mother Owl won't wake the sun so that the day can come."

Then the king called for the crow. That
big bird came flapping up. He said, "King
Lion, it was the rabbit's fault! I saw her
running for her life in the daytime. Wasn't
that reason enough to spread an alarm?"

The king nodded his head and said to the
council: "So, it was the rabbit who startled the
crow, who alarmed the monkey, who killed the
owlet—and now Mother Owl won't wake the
sun so that the day can come."

Then King Lion called the rabbit. "Rabbit,"
cried the king, "why did you break a law of
nature and go running, running, running, in
the daytime?"

"Oh, King," said the rabbit, "it was the python's fault. I was in my house when that big snake came in and chased me out."

The king said to the council: "So, it was the python who scared the rabbit, who startled the crow, who alarmed the monkey, who killed the owlet—and now Mother Owl won't wake the sun so that the day can come."

King Lion called the python, who came slithering, wasawusu, wasawusu, past the other animals. "But, King," he cried, "it was the iguana's fault! He wouldn't speak to me. I thought he was plotting some mischief against me. When I crawled into the rabbit's hole, I was only trying to hide."

The king said to the council: "So, it was the iguana who frightened the python, who scared the rabbit, who startled the crow, who alarmed the monkey, who killed the owlet— and now Mother Owl won't wake the sun so that the day can come."

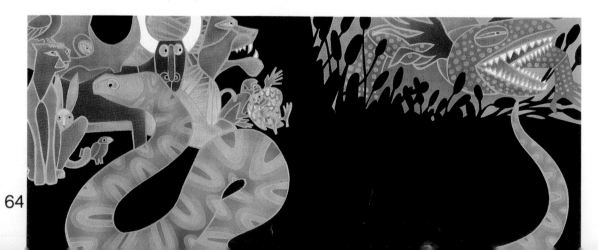

Now the iguana was not at the meeting. For he had not heard the call. The antelope was sent to get him. All the animals laughed when they saw the iguana coming, badamin, badamin, with the sticks still stuck in his ears!

King Lion pulled out the sticks, purup, purup. Then he asked, "Iguana, what evil have you been plotting against the python?"

"None! None at all!" cried the iguana. "Python is my friend!"

"Then why wouldn't you say good morning to me?" asked the snake.

"I didn't hear you, or even see you!" said the iguana. "Mosquito told me such a big lie, I couldn't bear to listen to it. So I put sticks in my ears. It was the mosquito's fault."

King Lion said to the council: "So, it was the mosquito who annoyed the iguana, who frightened the python, who scared the rabbit, who startled the crow, who alarmed the monkey, who killed the owlet—and now Mother Owl won't wake the sun so that the day can come."

"Punish the mosquito! Punish the mosquito!" cried all the animals.

When Mother Owl heard that, she was satisfied. She turned her head toward the east and hooted: "Hoo! Hooooo! Hoooooooo!"

And the sun came up.

To this day the mosquito goes about whining in people's ears: "Zeee! Is everyone still angry at me?"

When she does that, she gets an honest answer.

KPAO!

# Questions

1. Why did the iguana put sticks in his ears?

2. Why did King Lion call a meeting of the animals?

3. Do you agree that it was the mosquito's fault that one of Mother Owl's babies was killed? Why or why not?

4. The author used many words to describe sounds. Make up a word to describe a sound and tell what sound it describes.

## Applying Reading Skills
### Causes of an Event

Answer these questions on your paper about "Why Mosquitoes Buzz in People's Ears."

1. Why didn't the iguana speak to the python?
2. Why did the rabbit run out of her hole?
3. Why did the crow cry in the forest?
4. Why did the monkey begin screeching and leaping?
5. Why did the monkey land on the branch that killed Mother Owl's owlet?

# SKILLS activity

## CONTEXT CLUES

One way to figure out the meaning of a new word is to read the whole sentence in which the word is found. The other words become the clues. This is called "defining a word using context clues." The **context** is the rest of the sentence. The word you are defining from context must make sense in the sentence.

**ACTIVITY**  Read each story below. Use context clues to discover the meaning of the underlined word. Then, write the sentence with the word meaning on your paper.

The horse pulled the chariot. The chariot's wheels spinned. The chariot driver looked at the wheels.

1. A chariot is _____.
   an animal
   a two-wheeled cart
   a plant

A mosquito buzzed in my ear. I felt the mosquito bite me. The mosquito bite itched and itched.

2. A mosquito is _____.
   a python
   an insect
   a bird

I was so tired, I yawned. I stretched and yawned again. My mouth was wide open when I yawned.

3. When you yawn, you open your mouth because _____.

you are angry
you are sleepy
you are happy

Ann's dog had to be punished. The dog had chewed Ann's boot. Ann punished the dog by making it stay outside.

4. When you are punished, you have _____.
done something wrong
done something fair
made someone happy

The mother owl fed the owlets. The owlets were too small to fly. The owlets stayed in the nest.

5. An owlet is a _____.
father owl
home for owls
baby owl

# WHAT IS THAT ALLIGATOR SAYING?

Ruth Belov Gross

Except in stories like folk tales, animals do not talk to each other the way people do. But they do have ways of telling each other things. In this article, you will find out how some animals communicate.

Many kinds of baby animals cannot take care of themselves. They need their parents to feed them and to keep them safe.

These baby animals have special ways to tell their parents when they are hungry or in trouble. And the parents have special ways to warn the babies when there is danger.

Baby alligators communicate with their mothers by grunting. Whenever a mother alligator hears her babies grunting—*umph, umph, umph*—she comes to them right away.

The first time a mother alligator hears her babies, she cannot see them. Their little grunts are coming from a pile of mud and old leaves. That is where the mother alligator laid her eggs many weeks ago.

Now the mother alligator goes to the pile of leaves. She digs it open with her long alligator snout. There, under the leaves, are her babies! She helps them get out of their muddy nest.

A mother hen is with her chicks almost all the time. She keeps them warm under her feathers. She helps them find food. And she keeps them safe from other animals.

What makes the baby chicks and the mother hen stay together? They stay together because they "talk" to each other.

When the mother hen goes *cluck—cluck—cluck*, the chicks come running to her. When the chicks go *peep—peep—peep*, the mother hen comes to them.

Scientists did not always know what made a mother hen come to her chicks. Did she come to them because she saw them—or because she heard them?

One day a scientist made an experiment. He put a chick under a big glass bowl. The mother hen could see her chick but she could not hear it. No one outside the bowl could hear it.

*Peep—peep—peep* went the chick, but the mother hen walked right past the bowl.

Then the scientist put the chick behind a wooden fence. The mother hen could not see her chick behind the fence. But she could hear it.

*Peep–peep–peep* went the chick. The mother hen heard it and went straight to the fence.

The experiment showed the scientist that the mother hen came to her chicks because she heard them.

Animals cannot say "Watch out!" the way we can. They have their own ways of warning each other that danger may be near.

A beaver uses its tail to say "Watch out!" It lifts its tail up over its back. Then it smacks its tail *hard* on the water of the beaver pond.

The sound can be heard far away. It tells other beavers that an enemy is near.

When the other beavers hear the smacking sound, they dive into the pond. But first they smack *their* tails on the water.

Smack! Whack! Smack! The beavers are passing the danger signal along.

Crows are noisy birds. They go *caw—caw—caw* a lot, and they make other noises, too.

Hubert and Mable Frings are two scientists who studied "crow talk." They wanted to find out how crows tell each other "Watch out—danger! Fly away quickly!" They hid microphones near a bunch of crows, and they attached the microphones to a tape recorder.

After a while Dr. and Mrs. Frings had a lot of different crow sounds on their tapes. Then they played the sounds back to the crows over a loudspeaker. They played the sounds one at a time.

They played the first sound back to the crows. Nothing happened. They played another sound, and again nothing happened.

Then they tried a third sound. When they played this sound, crows came flying from all over.

They tried one more crow sound—and this time all the crows flew away! The crows flew away every time that sound was played.

Now Dr. and Mrs. Frings knew which sound meant "watch out—fly away." They named this the "alarm call."

They also knew which sound made the crows come together. They named this the "assembly call."

An ant has two feelers sticking out of the top of its head. It feels things with its feelers, and it smells things with them, too.

Ants use their feelers when they communicate with each other.

Sometimes an ant finds a piece of food that is too big to carry. The ant gets excited and runs back to its nest.

On the way, it stops many times. It presses its body against the ground and leaves a little spot of smelly stuff. The spots make a smelly trail on the ground.

When the ant gets back to its nest, the other ants rush to the smelly trail. They follow it with their feelers. The trail tells them, "This way to the food."

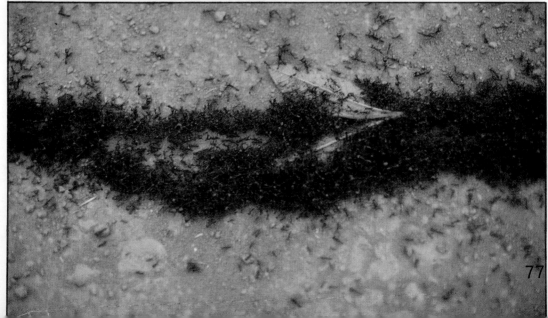

Other animals also have ways of telling each other there's food. Flies leave a special smell on the food they visit. The smell helps other flies find the food.

Here is an experiment someone tried. First he found a place where there were some flies. He put some sugar where the flies could get to it. Then he waited. After a long while, one fly found the sugar. But soon after that, many flies came.

Why did the other flies come? Did they smell the sugar? No—sugar does not have a smell.

They came because they smelled the fly smell on the sugar. Every fly that came to the sugar left some fly smell there.

These are just some of the ways animals communicate. You can find out more about animal communication by listening to animals and by watching what animals do. Maybe you will find out something that nobody knew before.

# Questions

1. How do mother alligators and mother hens find their babies?

2. Why did Hubert and Mable Frings play the crow sounds they had taped back to the crows?

3. Do you think ants or flies have a better way of telling other ants and flies where there is food? Why?

4. What experiment could you do to learn about the way a dog or cat communicates?


## Applying Reading Skills
### Recall Details

Think about "What Is That Alligator Saying?". Try to remember some of the important details about the story. Use complete sentences to answer these questions.

1. How do baby alligators communicate with their mothers?

2. Where does the mother alligator lay her eggs?

3. What does a beaver use to warn other beavers of danger?

4. What two ways do ants use to find food?

# Off for a Hike

My puppy can't speak English,
she doesn't know a letter,
but her wiggles and her wriggles
when she sees me get my sweater
and her raggle-taggle waggles
when I pack a lunch and pet her
are just as good as talking is . . .
and maybe even better.

Aileen Fisher

# The Parrot Who Wouldn't Say "Cataño"

Pura Belpré

Parrots are unusual birds. In a way,
they *can* talk like we do. They are able to
repeat people's words. But they do not
understand the words. As you will see,
the man in this folk tale has trouble
communicating with his companion, a
parrot.

$\mathbb{A}$cross the bay from San Juan in Puerto Rico is a town called Cataño. Here, long ago, lived a retired sailor called Yuba. His only companion was a parrot—a beautiful, talkative bird known to all the town. Much as the parrot talked, there was one thing she refused to say. That was the name of the town. No matter how hard Yuba tried to teach her, she would never say the word. This saddened Yuba who loved his town very much.

"You are an ungrateful bird," Yuba told the parrot. "You repeat everything you hear, yet refuse to say the name of the town where you have lived most of your life." But all the parrot would do was to blink her eyes and talk of other things.

One day as Yuba sat on his balcony with the parrot on his knee, who should come by but Don Casimiro, the rich poultry breeder from San Juan. He stopped and listened. In all his years he had never heard such a parrot. What a wonderful addition to his poultry yard she would make! The more he listened to her conversation, the more he wanted to own her.

"Would you sell me that parrot?" he said at last. "I will pay you well for her."

"Neither silver nor gold can buy her, Señor," said Yuba.

Don Casimiro was surprised. This man looked as if he could use some money. "What else would you take for her, my good man?" he asked.

"Nothing. But I will make a bargain with you," replied Yuba.

"A bargain? What kind of a bargain?" Don Casimiro wanted to know.

"I have been trying to teach her to say 'Cataño.' But for reasons of her own she refuses to say it. Well, take her with you."

"If you can make her say it, the bird is
yours and I will be grateful to you for the rest
of my life. If you fail, bring her back to me."

"Agreed," said Don Casimiro delightedly.
He took the parrot, thanked Yuba, and left.

Late that afternoon he returned home. He
sat in the corridor facing the courtyard filled
with fancy fowls and potted plants. "Now," he
said to the parrot, "repeat after me: *Ca-ta-ño!*"
He took great care to say each syllable clearly
and slowly. The parrot flapped her wings, but
said not a word.

"Come, come," said Don Casimiro. "Say *Ca-ta-ño*." The parrot blinked her eyes at him, but said not a word.

"But you can say anything you want. I have heard you speak. Let's try it again. *Ca-ta-ño*." Don Casimiro waited, but the parrot walked away down the corridor as if she hadn't heard him.

Now Don Casimiro was a man of great wealth, but little patience. His temper was as hot as the chili peppers he grew in his vegetable patch. He went after the parrot who had stopped beside a large potted plant at the end of the corridor. He grabbed the bird. "Say *CA-TA-ÑO!*" he commanded.

The parrot blinked and quickly wriggled herself out of his hands. But Don Casimiro picked her up again and held her fast. "Say *Ca-ta-ño*, or I will throw you out of the window!"

The parrot said not a word.

Blinded with anger, Don Casimiro threw her out of the window. The parrot landed in the chicken coop.

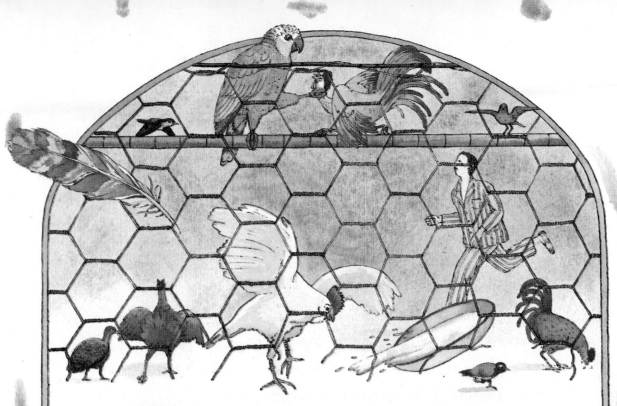

That night a strange noise rose from the courtyard. Don Casimiro awoke with a start. "Thieves!" he cried.

Thinking they were after his fowls he rushed out of the house and headed for the chicken coop. What a turmoil! Chicken feathers flew every which way. Pails of water and chicken feed were overturned. Squawking chickens ran around in circles.

Suddenly, from the far end of the coop rose a voice saying: "Say *Ca-ta-ño*, or I will throw you out of the window!"

There, sitting on a rafter, was the parrot, clutching one of the most prized fowls. Don Casimiro rushed to the spot and pulled the parrot down.

Before the sun had risen he was on the ferryboat on the way to Yuba's home. The parrot sat on his knees as if she had forgotten the happenings of the night before. He found Yuba sitting on his balcony.

"So you failed, too," said Yuba sadly.

"Oh, no, no!" Don Casimiro replied. "She said 'Cataño' all right! But the bargain is off. I want you to take her back."

Yuba was puzzled.

on Casimiro noticed his confusion and quickly added: "You see, she made a mess of my chicken house before she said 'Cataño.'"

Yuba's face shone with happiness. He took the parrot and held her close. He watched Don Casimiro hurrying down the street toward the ferryboat station.

"Say *Ca-ta-ño*," he whispered to the parrot.

"Cataño, Cataño," the parrot replied.

And since that day no one was happier, in all of Cataño, than Yuba the retired sailor.

## Questions

1. What bargain did Yuba make with Don Casimiro?

2. Why do you think the parrot messed up Don Casimiro's chicken house?

3. Do you think Yuba will ever make a bargain to give away his parrot again?

4. If you had a pet, what trick would you teach it? How would you do it?

## Applying Reading Skills
### Recall Details

Think about "The Parrot Who Wouldn't Say 'Cataño.'" Try to remember some of these important details about the story. Use complete sentences to answer these questions.

1. Where is the town of Cataño?

2. What work did Don Casimiro do?

3. What did Don Casimiro grow in his vegetable garden?

4. Where did the parrot land when Don Casimiro threw her out of the window?

# Pura Belpré

"I grew up in a family of storytellers. My vivid imagination and photographic mind kept scenes that impressed me as a child very alive. The color and delicate scent of a flower . . . the chant of the vendors on their way to the market . . ."

When Pura Belpré came to New York City from Puerto Rico, those scenes of childhood stayed with her. As a librarian, she enjoyed telling tales to children. But when Belpré looked for folk tales from her native land, she didn't find a single book. "To see these tales in book form with the other ones on the shelves became my dream," she has said. A story Belpré wrote for a storytelling class was shown to a publisher. It became her first book, *Perez and Martina.*

**More to Read**   *Oté: A Puerto Rican Folk Tale*
*The Dance of the Animals*

# Koko's Kitten

Dr. Francine Patterson
Photographs by Dr. Ronald H. Cohn

Some animals really can communicate
with people, if we can find the right way
to ask them. In 1972, Dr. Francine
Patterson began to teach a baby female
gorilla named Koko how to communicate.
She taught her American Sign Language—
the language used by deaf people—in
which hand, face, and body movements are
used to stand for words.

When Dr. Patterson asked Koko what
she wanted for her twelfth birthday, Koko
signed "cat." Dr. Patterson—with help from
Koko—will tell you the rest of the story.

I wasn't surprised that Koko asked for a cat for her birthday. I have been reading to Koko for many years. Two of her favorite stories have been "Puss in Boots" and "The Three Little Kittens."

Koko gets very interested in the stories I read her. When reading the story of the three little kittens who lose their mittens, Koko sees that their mother is angry. She notices that the kittens are crying.

"Mad," Koko signs.

Koko loves picture books. Gorilla books are her favorites. Cat books are next. She likes to go off on her own with a book. She will look at the pictures and sign to herself.

On her birthday, I gave Koko the usual presents. She got apple juice and some special fruits and nuts. She got a baby doll, too. I didn't want to give Koko a stuffed toy. I knew she'd eventually destroy it.

The only durable cat toy I could find was in a mail order catalogue. I ordered it right away. It was made of cement and covered with vinyl and black velvet. I decided on it because it looked real. It was strong—gorilla–proof. The toy cat didn't come in time for Koko's birthday. So I decided to save it for Christmas.

In December, I made a list for Koko. I drew about twenty pictures. "What do you want for Christmas?" I asked as I showed Koko the pictures.

Koko carefully looked at the book. Then she pointed to a doll, nuts—and a cat.

I bought Koko some nuts and a new doll. I wrapped the toy cat. I put it with the rest of her presents.

On Christmas morning, Koko ate her cereal. Then she opened her stocking. It was filled with nuts. Koko threw the nuts aside. She went to her next present.

Koko unwrapped the velvet cat. "That red," she signed.

Koko often uses the word red to express anger. Koko was very upset. She started running back and forth, banging on her walls.

It is natural for gorillas to do this when frightened or in great danger. But this was Christmas. It was usually a happy day for Koko, and she was with people she loved.

I finally understood Koko's strange behavior. She was unhappy with her Christmas present. I had made a mistake. Koko did not want a cement and velvet toy cat. Koko wanted a real cat. Koko wanted a pet.

Things don't always happen as quickly as we would like them to. Every day is full of its own activities. So it was almost six months later when Karen, one of my assistants, came with three kittens.

Karen showed the kittens to Koko.

"Love that," Koko signed.

"Which one do you want?" we asked.

"That," signed Koko, pointing to the gray tabby.

I am not sure why Koko picked the gray tabby as her favorite. I never asked her. Perhaps it was because he didn't have a tail. A gorilla has no tail.

That night, all three kittens went home with Karen. Two days later, the kittens came back for another visit. Koko was happy to see them.

"Visit love tiger cat," Koko signed.

First she picked up the gray and white one. Then Koko took the tailless tabby. She carried him on her thigh. After a while, she pushed him up onto the back of her neck.

"Baby," Koko signed.

She cradled the tabby in her legs. She examined its paws. Koko squeezed, and the tabby's claws came out.

"Cat do scratch," Koko signed. "Koko love."

"What will you name the kitty?" I asked.

"All Ball," Koko signed.

"Yes," I said. "Like a ball, he has no tail."

Ball stayed overnight as a visiting kitten. By the end of the week, Ball was a permanent member of our household.

Koko had her kitten at last.

For the first few weeks, Ball lived in my house. Every evening at six o'clock, I would take Ball to Koko's trailer for an evening visit. I carried the kitten in my pocket as I got Koko ready for bed. Koko soon grew used to this routine.

"What happens at night?" I asked.

"All Ball," signed Koko.

"Right," I said. "Ball visits you at night."

When he was older, Ball would go into Koko's trailer by himself. It worried me at first. I did not know how Koko would treat the kitten alone. As it turned out, Koko was always gentle. Ball was never afraid of her.

Koko was a good gorilla mother. She combed and petted Ball to keep him clean. She also looked at his eyes, ears, and mouth to make sure he was healthy.

Ball was often a topic of conversation during Koko's lessons.

"Love visit," Koko signed when Ball and I arrived for a morning lesson.

Koko seemed to enjoy conversations about her kitten. This conversation took place between Koko and a research assistant named Janet.

"I'll give you some grapes if you tell me about Ball, the cat," Janet said.

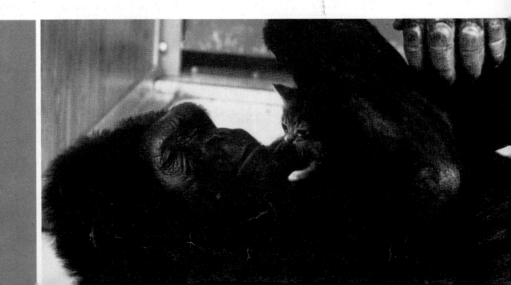

"Soft," Koko signed.

"What kind of animal is he?" Janet asked.

"Cat, cat, cat," Koko answered.

"Do you love Ball?"

"Soft, good cat cat," Koko signed.

Besides sign language, art is another way I test Koko. Ball lay with a green toy on an orange towel. I gave Koko a canvas and some paints. Then I asked her to draw Ball. Koko had ten colors to choose from. First she picked black for Ball's body. Next she picked orange for the towel. Then she picked green for the toy.

"What about Ball's eyes?" I asked.

Koko picked tan.

On a foggy December morning, one of the assistants told me that Ball had been hit by a car. He had died at once.

I was shocked and unprepared. I didn't know how close I had grown to Ball. I had no idea how the news would affect Koko. The kitten meant so much to her. He was Koko's baby.

I went to Koko at once. I told her that Ball had been hit by a car. She would not see him again.

Koko did not respond. I thought she didn't understand, so I left the trailer.

Ten minutes later, I heard Koko cry. It was her distress call. She gave a loud, long series of high-pitched hoots.

Three days later, Koko and I had a conversation about Ball.

"Do you want to talk about your kitty?" I asked.

"Cry," Koko signed.

"Can you tell me more about it?" I asked.

"Blind," she signed.

"We don't see him anymore, do we? What happened to your kitty?" I asked.

"Sleep cat," Koko signed.

News of All Ball's death traveled quickly. We got thousands of letters. People of all ages wrote to us. They all had one message. Koko should have a new kitten.

In January, I showed Koko a picture of three kittens. One had a long tail. One had a short tail. One was tailless.

"When you get another kitty, what kind would you like?" I asked.

"That," Koko signed as she pointed to the tailless cat.

"We'll get you a kitty like that," I said. "Is that okay?"

"Good. Nice," Koko answered.

"How do you feel about kitties?" I asked.

"Cat gorilla have visit," she signed. "Koko love."

Koko was ready for a new kitten. Now if only I could find one.

More time went by. I called the Humane Society. They had no kittens at all—let alone a rare, tailless Manx. I called many other places. I was disappointed again and again.

Then our luck changed. We got a letter from a breeder of Manx cats. He wanted to help. He didn't have any kittens then, but he called other Manx breeders. At last he found a litter of Manx kittens in Southern California. They were just about ready to leave their mother.

Finally, on March 24, a red, tiger-striped Manx was brought to our home. Seeing the kitten, Koko purred with joy. It was a wonderful moment. She placed him on her chest and petted him.

"Let me hold the kitty," I said.

But Koko would not let go. She kissed and cradled her kitten.

"Baby," she signed.

Koko was happy. Her new kitten had come to stay.

## Questions

1. What did Koko do when she was given a toy cat? Why?

2. Why did Dr. Patterson only let Koko visit with All Ball for short periods in the beginning?

3. How would you compare the way Koko reacted to All Ball's death to the way a person might react if his or her pet died?

4. If you had a chance to meet Koko, what would you ask her?

## Applying Reading Skills
### Follow Directions

Koko learned to communicate by following her trainer's directions. Follow these directions on your paper.

Draw a cat toy for Koko.

Draw a circle around the toy.

Draw a triangle to the right of the toy.

Now write your own set of directions in three steps for making a cat toy.

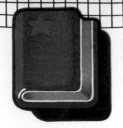

# SKILLS activity

## FOLLOW DIRECTIONS

When you are learning to do something for the first time, you need to follow the directions. You should read all of the directions before you begin. Then you should follow each step in order. Be sure not to skip any directions.

**ACTIVITY A**   Read the story. Then follow the directions.

When you train an animal to do something, you have to show it what to do over and over again. Training a parrot to talk is not easy. You must get the parrot to look at you and listen. Then you must say the same thing over and over again. You must reward the parrot if it says the right thing.

1. Write a list of three things you would train a parrot to say.
2. Say each thing on the list twenty times.
3. Draw a picture of the parrot saying the first thing on your list. Make it look as if the words are coming out of the parrot's mouth.

My feathers are beautiful!
My feathers are beautiful!
My feathers are beautiful!
My feathers are beautiful!
My feathers are beautiful!

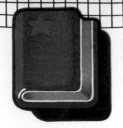

104

**ACTIVITY B** Scientists study animals to try to understand how and why they act as they do. A scientist who wants to know something about an animal must watch the animal for days and days. Often students help the scientists do this kind of study. The students must follow directions very carefully. They must write down everything the animal does.

Pretend you are a scientist interested in when animals eat during the day. Follow the directions below.

1. Choose an animal that you have seen often. It could be a pet or a familiar animal like a squirrel or even a common bird like a blue jay. Write the name of the animal at the top of your paper.
2. Make a chart that shows every hour of the day.
3. Now pretend that you are watching everything the animal is eating. Every time the animal eats, in your imagination, make a check on the chart. If you know what kinds of food your animal eats, write the food next to the check.

Your chart might look like this:

| Times the Animal Eats | | |
|---|---|---|
| 6:00 AM | | 9:00 |
| 7:00 AM | ✓ birdseed | 10:00 |
| 8:00 AM | | 11:00 |

105

# The Code in the Mailbox

### Kathy Kennedy Tapp

*Dr. Patterson and Koko used sign language to communicate with each other. Sometimes people use secret languages, or codes, to communicate. That's what Tad, the boy in this story, does when he plays detective with his friend. One day, instead of playing detective, Tad has to help a neighbor with a special need move in across the street. He never expected he would discover a new way to send a secret message. Find out what kind of code Tad puts in his neighbor's mailbox.*

"I don't want to go," Tad said for the third time.

His mother faced him, hands on hips. "Tad, I'm ashamed of you. Mr. James is blind and needs help getting settled. I told him you'd be over."

"Mom, it's Easter vacation. I was going to meet Perry. We made plans."

"More detective stuff, I'll bet." Michelle looked up from the egg she was poking with a pin. "Fingerprints . . . secret codes—"

Tad glared at his sister. "Just stick to your egg blowing, O.K.?"

"Codes are fine," Mom said. "But don't let me catch you using the mailbox across the street for your messages any more. It's Mr. James's mailbox now."

"I know," Tad muttered.

"And Mr. James needs help unpacking. Now scoot. We'll save the egg decorating until you get back."

So much for his plans to go through the new code book with Perry. Tad kicked a rock across the street. It skipped past the beautiful silver mailbox with the door and the signal flag he and Perry always raised when they left secret messages for each other.

A low voice answered Tad's knock. "Are you Tad?"

"Yes."

"Come on in. Careful of the boxes."

The room was dark with the drapes closed. Boxes lined the walls. Tad stayed by the door, trying to ignore the butterflies in his stomach. Being around somebody who couldn't see made him feel nervous.

"We'll start over here," Mr. James said, walking toward the wall, one arm out in front. His foot hit a box and he reached down inside it. "Pans. They go in the kitchen. Next box should be plates—"

The old man went through box after box.
He didn't talk except to give instructions. Tad
made fifty trips down the dark hall. One more
box. Just one more—

"Where do these go?" he asked.

"Books. Leave them for now. Shelves aren't
up yet."

"Books?" Tad stared. He'd never seen books
like these before. Big pads of thick pages all
covered with bumps.

Braille. Of course. He pulled one out,
feeling the dots. Did those bumps really make
words? How could anyone read them?

109

"Mr. James, did you learn Braille in school?"

"No need then. I learned the regular alphabet, just like you."

Tad set down the book. "You mean . . . you weren't blind when you were a kid?" he stammered.

"I could throw and catch with the best of them. What about you? You play ball?"

"I play basketball in the winter. Now I'm busy with other stuff. Detective stuff."

"Detective, huh? Fingerprints, spyglasses—that sort of thing?"

"And codes. I like codes best." Tad was still fingering the Braille bumps. "Can anyone learn Braille?"

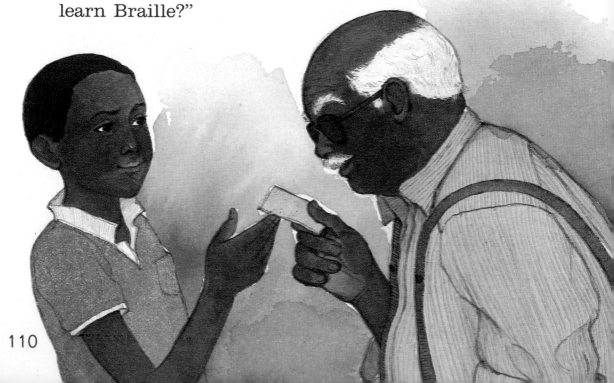

"Anyone willing to spend enough time."
Mr. James started to feel around in the book
box. "Here it is." Mr. James held up a little
card. "A Braille alphabet card."

"Can I borrow it?"

"I don't need it anymore," Mr. James said,
shaking his head and grinning a little.
"Detectives. That's a new one. Spring was
baseball time when I was a kid. I was team
captain. 'Babe' they called me."

"Babe?" Tad grinned, too. "What was your
average?"

"Well—" Mr. James chewed his lip a
second. "Let's just say it was a lot better than
I could do now."

Mr. James got up. "That's enough work
for today. It's getting late." He pulled out his
wallet, and Tad noticed that some bills were
folded the long way and others the short way.
Mr. James fingered them, then held one out to
Tad. "Thanks for your help."

A five! Tad stood there, twisting the bill in
his hand. A five—just for unloading some
boxes. "Thanks. Uh . . . have a happy Easter."

Crossing the street, Tad thought about the new detective stuff he would buy with his five dollars.

"You're back just in time," Mom greeted him. "The eggs are ready to go. Michelle's done a few already."

Batik egg-dyeing was a tradition at their house. The designs were drawn on the eggs in pencil first, then traced with nails dipped in hot wax. When the eggs were dyed, the waxed designs remained white.

"Of course *you* wouldn't appreciate it. It's not in *code* or anything," Michelle said.

Code. Tad fingered the little wax bumps on the egg, remembering the Braille card in his pocket.

"Be back in a minute." He grabbed an egg on his way to the bedroom and shut the door. He'd pencil it in here, then do the wax part in the kitchen. Dots weren't hard at all.

He studied the alphabet. The card said that six dots make up a Braille cell, like this and that each letter of the Braille alphabet is formed by a different arrangement of the dots. What a code!

**B    A    B    E**

There! He did it on paper first, then on the eggshell.

"That's a design?" Michelle cried when he set the finished egg on the rack carefully, each letter dotted in wax.

"A lot you know," Tad answered.

At 10:15 the next morning, right after the letter carrier made his Saturday delivery, Tad crouched behind the tree in Mr. James's yard, waiting.

Fifteen minutes later the cane tip-tapped down the walkway. Tad hardly breathed as Mr. James pulled the egg out of the mailbox.

Were the wax dots close enough? Were they in the right position for B-A-B-E? Tad felt ready to explode, watching, waiting.

Mr. James's face wrinkled as his fingers turned the egg over and over in his hand. Suddenly he smiled. He leaned back against the mailbox, still fingering the egg.

Finally Mr. James put the egg carefully into his shirt pocket and picked up his cane. Not like a cane, but like a baseball bat! With both hands gripping below the curve, he pulled back and swung.

Tad crept away, feeling a bit embarrassed, but proud, too.

Case of the code in the mailbox—closed.

## Questions

1. Why did Tad have to go to Mr. James's house?

2. Why was Tad interested in Mr. James's Braille books?

3. Why do you think Tad put the egg in Mr. James's mailbox instead of giving it to him in person?

4. Make up a simple code. Write a message to a friend using your code.

## Applying Reading Skills
### Context Clues

Read the sentences below. Use context clues to choose the meaning of each underlined word. Then write each word and its meaning.

1. Tad didn't want to listen to his sister, so he ignored her.
   a. watched          b. paid no attention to
   c. treated unkindly  d. made better

2. Mr. James appreciated what Tad did for him because he said, "Thanks for your help."
   a. was thankful      b. approved of
   c. kept away from    d. uncovered

115

# MAXIE

## MILDRED KANTROWITZ

Sometimes you can learn about your
neighbors just by listening. When you wake
up in the morning, what sounds do you hear?
A dog barking? A baby crying? Listening is
an important part of communicating and
understanding the world around you. The
neighbors in this story listen very carefully to
Maxie's morning sounds.

Maxie lived in three small rooms on the top floor of an old brownstone house on Orange Street. She had lived there for many years, and every day was the same for Maxie.

Every morning, seven days a week, every morning at exactly seven o'clock, Maxie raised the shades on her three front windows. Every morning at exactly 7:10, Maxie's large, orange cat jumped up onto the middle windowsill and sprawled there in the morning sun.

At 7:20, if you were watching Maxie's back window, you could see her raise the shade to the very top. Then she uncovered a bird cage. On the perch inside the cage was a yellow canary. He was waiting for his water dish to be filled. It always was, if you were still watching, at 7:22.

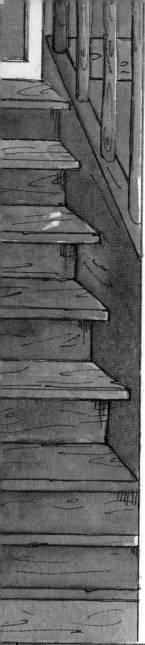

At 8:15 every morning, Maxie's door
opened with a tired squeak. Maxie's old,
leather slippers made slapping sounds as she
walked down the four flights of uncarpeted
stairs to the front door. Outside the front door
were the bottles of milk in a container. Maxie
always tried to hold the door open with her
left foot while she reached out to get her milk.
But every morning it was just a little too far
for her to reach. The door always banged shut
and locked behind her.

So, at 8:20 every morning, Maxie rang the
bell marked "Superintendent." The
superintendent, whose name was Arthur,
would open the door for Maxie and let her in
with her milk.

Only Maxie and the woman at the grocery
store knew what she ate for breakfast, but
everyone knew she drank tea. At 8:45 every
morning, they could hear the whistling of her
tea kettle. How Maxie loved that whistle! She

loved it so much that she let it sing out for one full minute. Dogs howled, cats whined, and babies bawled, but everyone knew that when the whistle stopped, it would be 8:46. And it always was.

The letter carrier knew more about Maxie than anyone else did. He knew that she had a sister in Chicago who sent her a Christmas card every year. He also knew when Maxie planted the flowers in her window boxes because every spring he delivered her seed catalog. Then a few weeks later he delivered packets of seeds.

Every morning at nine o'clock, Maxie walked down the stairs for the second time in her leather slippers. She went outside and put her small bag of garbage in the pail on the front stoop. Then she came back in and waited for the letter carrier. She walked slowly past him in the hall, watching him put mail in the slots for the other people who lived in the house.

Then she climbed the four flights of stairs again, resting at each landing. When she got to the top, Maxie went into her apartment. The door closed after her with the same tired squeak.

One afternoon at 1:05, just as she did every afternoon at 1:05, Maxie moved the bird cage with the yellow bird in it to the front windows. It was shady and cool there now.

The large, orange cat moved to the back window and sprawled there, soaking up the sun that matched the color of his fur.

"You're perfectly happy just lying there, day after day," Maxie said to the cat. "All you ever want to do is move from one window to the other and watch the world go by. You don't need anyone, and no one really needs you. But you don't seem to care."

Maxie turned away from the window. "I care," she said sadly. "I'm not a cat. But I might as well be." Maxie felt very tired, and she went to bed. That was Monday.

On Tuesday morning at seven o'clock, the three shades on Maxie's front windows and the one on her back window remained down. At 7:10, the large, orange cat was still asleep at the foot of Maxie's bed.

And at 7:30, there were no sweet warbling sounds. That morning no one heard the sounds of Maxie's leather slippers on the stairs. Her tea kettle was filled with empty silence.

At nine o'clock, the letter carrier came with the daily mail. He had a seed catalog for Maxie and he waited for her to come down the stairs. Since she didn't come and this was most unusual, he decided to deliver the catalog to her door.

He climbed the four flights of stairs. He knocked and waited. There was no sign of Maxie.

At 9:03, Mr. Turkle, who lived on the third floor, came hurrying up the stairs. At 9:05, Mr. and Mrs. Moorehouse got there from across the street. At 9:07, Mrs. Garcia came over from next door. Susie Smith came up at 9:10 with her twin brothers.

Five members of the family on the second floor made it up by 9:13. Then came Arthur, the superintendent. By 9:17, there were seventeen people, three dogs and two cats, all waiting for Maxie to open the door.

And when she didn't they all went in. They found Maxie in bed. More people came up the stairs and someone called a doctor. By the time she got there, there were forty-two grown-ups and eleven children in Maxie's small living room.

When the doctor came out of Maxie's bedroom she shook her head sadly. "Maxie isn't really sick," she said. "She's lonely. She doesn't feel loved. She doesn't feel that anyone needs her."

No one said anything for a minute. Then suddenly Mrs. Garcia got up and walked right past the doctor and into the bedroom. "Maxie!" she shouted angrily, "you let me down. You and that warbling bird let me down!"

"Every morning I wake up when I hear that bird. Then it's my job to wake my husband. He has the morning shift at the corner diner and he's still asleep. Why, there must be at least seventy-five people at that diner right now, waiting for their breakfasts. They'll all have to go to work on empty stomachs—all because of you and that yellow bird!"

Everyone else crowded into the bedroom. Maxie sat up in bed and listened to what they had to say. "I couldn't go to school this morning," Susie Smith said. "I missed my bus because I didn't hear your tea kettle whistle."

"The school bus never came this morning," said Mr. Turkle who drove the bus. "I didn't wake up in time. I never heard Sarah Sharpe's footsteps on my ceiling."

Sarah Sharpe was a nurse who lived just above Mr. Turkle. There were a lot of people waiting for her right now at the hospital. She always got up when she heard Maxie's door squeak.

Mr. and Mrs. Moorehouse both had very important jobs but they had missed their train that morning. Their alarm clock was Maxie's window shade. Arthur said he hadn't swept the front steps that morning. He overslept because Maxie didn't ring his bell. He hoped no one would complain. They all talked about it and decided that there must be about four hundred people who needed Maxie—or who needed someone else who needed Maxie—every morning.

Maxie smiled. She got out of bed and made a pot of tea. In fact, she made five pots of tea. Each time the kettle whistled, dogs howled, cats whined, and babies bawled, Maxie listened and thought about how many people were being touched by these sounds—her sounds. By 9:45 that morning, Maxie had served tea to everybody, and she was so pleased.

# Questions

1. What were three things Maxie did each morning?
2. Why did Maxie stay in bed on Tuesday morning?
3. Do you think Maxie's life will be different from now on? Why or why not?
4. What are some sounds you hear in the morning?

## Applying Reading Skills
### Causes of an Event

Think about the story "Maxie" and write the answers to these questions.

1. Why did Mr. and Mrs. Moorehouse miss their train?
2. Why didn't Susie Smith go to school that morning?
3. Why did Maxie stay in bed on Tuesday morning?

# SKILLS activity

## PARTS OF A BOOK

An **index** is an alphabetical list that is used for finding information. An index can contain names, subjects, dates, or places. An index is often found at the end of a book. A book about birds might have an index that lists all the birds in the book in alphabetical order. After each bird, the index would show the page number where that bird is discussed in the book.

**ACTIVITY A**   Read this part of an index from a book about detectives. Then answer the questions.

cases, famous, 21          fingerprints, 14
cases, unsolved, 23        secrets, 54
codes, 76                  spyglasses, 119

1. Facts about codes can be found on page

   _____.

2. Where would you look up information about famous cases?
3. What subject is written about on page 14?
4. Would you find unsolved cases discussed before or after famous cases?
5. How would you find out what spyglasses are used for?

A **glossary** is a kind of dictionary. There is a glossary at the back of this book. It has some important words you have read in this book. The glossary tells you how to divide a word into its parts. It tells you how to say the word. It also tells you what the word means.

**ACTIVITY B**  Look up each word below in the glossary. Write the parts of each word on your paper. Then write the meaning of each word.

1. batik
2. delivery
3. arrangement
4. position
5. sprawled
6. canary
7. patience
8. ignore

After you have learned about these words, finish the following sentences with words from the list. Write the sentences on your paper.

The _____ man gave me a big package.
Sandy _____ across the bed and read her book.
The flower _____ looked pretty.
He couldn't _____ the loud noise.
The dress was made with a _____ design.
Her favorite _____ was first base.
Grandma showed a lot of _____ with her two-year-old grandchild.

# the Conversation Club

## Diane Stanley

Maxie learned that her neighbors depended upon her. They listened to her morning sounds. The members of the Conversation Club, however, never listen to one another.

When Peter Fieldmouse moved into his new house, Charlie came right over to welcome him. He told Peter about his new neighbors and about the Conversation Club they had. Peter had never heard of such a club. But before long, he became the club's listening expert.

"I want to invite you to join our club. I know you'll fit right in," Charlie said.

"Club?" asked Peter. He had never belonged to a club before. It might be fun, but he wasn't so sure he would fit right in.

"It's the Conversation Club. We meet every Thursday afternoon. Oh, we are a great group, let me tell you."

Charlie began to wave his arms excitedly. "Now, Sam, he knows everything about cooking—French cooking, Chinese cooking, you name it. Fay is our space expert. The planets, the stars, she'll tell you all about them. Pearl tells ghost stories."

Charlie turned and looked out the open door. "I'm the gardening expert. For example, I could tell you now that you ought to be getting your spring bulbs planted right away.

"Nancy speaks on sports. Right now she's doing football, and in the spring it's baseball, and so on. What's your subject?"

"I don't think I have a subject," Peter said.

"Nonsense! Of course you do!" shouted Charlie.

"Excuse me, the water is boiling for my tea," said Peter, backing toward his kitchen.

Peter took two cups from the shelf and, after adding tea to the boiling water, poured it carefully through a strainer into the cups.

"Couldn't I just listen?" suggested Peter.

Charlie seemed to be turning this idea over in his mind. "Stupendous idea!" he said at last.

"You can be the expert on listening. Oh, I really like that. Very original!"

"Thank you," said Peter shyly.

"So that's settled. The next meeting is Thursday at my house. Just ask anyone how to get there. Well, now I'm off. Things to do; places to go."

Peter was the last to arrive at Charlie's house on Thursday. As he removed his coat and muffler he saw that everyone was busy getting ready for the meeting to start.

"Hi, Peter," Charlie called. "Hey, everybody, this is Peter, our listening expert."

"Welcome, welcome," said another club member in a blue football jersey.

"You must be Nancy," said Peter.

"See," yelled Charlie, "didn't I say he was a listening expert?"

At last Charlie tapped on the table. "Are we ready?" he asked.

They all nodded yes.

"Then let us begin."

The conversation began very softly, like a low buzzing. As it grew louder and louder, Peter could scarcely believe his ears. Everyone in the room was talking at once!

It sounded something like this:

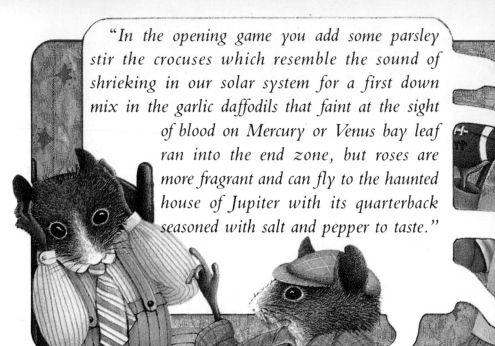

*"In the opening game you add some parsley stir the crocuses which resemble the sound of shrieking in our solar system for a first down mix in the garlic daffodils that faint at the sight of blood on Mercury or Venus bay leaf ran into the end zone, but roses are more fragrant and can fly to the haunted house of Jupiter with its quarterback seasoned with salt and pepper to taste."*

When he could stand it no longer, Peter ran to the door, opened it, and bolted into the cold, clear, quiet afternoon.

Behind him, the room quite suddenly grew still, and then everyone rushed out of Charlie's house, astonished.

"Where are you going? What's wrong?" they all cried. "Come back!"

"I can't," said Peter, stopping. "It gives me a headache. You all talk at the same time!"

"But we all have such interesting things to say," Nancy said.

Peter looked at them all, took a deep breath and said, "Yes, I'm sure that you do. But I can't be in your club because I have a club of my own."

"What kind of club? Who's in it? Can I join?" they all asked together.

"It's a listening club; no one talks, and I am the only member."

Peter began to walk home. He wrapped his muffler around his neck.

"Wait! Oh, wait! Can't we join? Oh, please, next week can we come to your house? I can't wait. How exciting. Another club!" they all said at once.

"Well, I guess so. But you have to obey the rules. No talking." Then he disappeared down the path.

Pearl watched him go. "You know what?" she said to the others. "Our conversation gives me a headache, too."

On the next Thursday, snow had been
falling all morning. The wind blew it against
the few dry leaves still on the trees and made
a rattling sound. In the quiet, Peter got the
tea things ready. The room smelled of newly
baked muffins.

They all came in together, along with a
gust of cold air. They chattered excitedly as
they hung up their coats and hats and
mufflers. Peter poured tea and passed the
steaming muffins as the club members found
chairs and moved closer to the fire.

The room began to feel warm again. There
were soft slurps and swallowing sounds.

"Are we doing this right?" Sam asked at
last.

"Oh, just great," Peter said.

Quietly Charlie said, "You know, I can't help thinking about the bulbs I planted. I planted them in the meadow instead of around the house. In the spring, while there is still snow, there will be yellow and purple crocuses."

"Oh, how beautiful that will be," said Peter, imagining it in his mind.

"Shhh!" said Nancy.

"Quiet!" said Sam.

They all had more tea. The wind outside blew in heavy gusts against the house.

"Did you know," said Fay, "that the Great Red Spot on Jupiter is really a giant storm that blows in a circle? It is thirty thousand miles long and has been blowing for over three hundred years!"

"Wow!" said Peter. "Three hundred years!"

The wind began to howl in the chimney. The windows rattled. But it was warm around the fire. "My house is nicer with friends in it," thought Peter. *Screetch*, went the branch on the window pane, *rattle, rattle, rattle.*

"What a perfect setting for the ghost story I wrote last night," said Pearl.

"Well, you can't tell it," said Fay.

"I know, but I can't help thinking . . ."

"This is a listening club, not a thinking club," said Nancy.

"It's my club," said Peter, "and I just changed the rules. Let Pearl tell her story, and everyone else will listen. Just one at a time—that's the new rule."

So while the snow whirled outside the little house and the wind howled, the friends all listened while Pearl told her story. It was the best they had ever heard.

## Questions

1.  What did Peter say he wanted to do if he joined the Conversation Club?

2.  What was wrong with the Conversation Club?

3.  Do you think the friends will continue the Listening Club? Why or why not?

4.  If you were to join a Conversation Club, what would be your subject? What would you talk about?

## Applying Reading Skills
### Realism and Fantasy

Write the headings on your paper:

>    *Could Happen*      *Could Only Happen in a Fantasy*

Then write each of the following sentences under the proper heading.

A field mouse moved to a new house.

Peter Fieldmouse joined a Conversation Club.

The girl in my club was the listening expert.

The children listened to the teacher.

The animals hung up their coats and mufflers.

# THE OTHER WAY TO LISTEN

I used to know
an old man
who could
walk
by any
cornfield
and hear
the corn
singing.

"Teach me,"
I'd say
when we'd
passed on by.
(I never said
a word
while he was
listening.)

"Just tell me
how
you learned
to hear
that
corn."

And he'd say,
"It takes
a lot of
practice.
You can't
be
in a hurry."

And I'd say,
"I have
the time."

He was so
good
at listening—
once
he heard
wildflower seeds
burst open,
beginning
to grow
underground.

That's hard to do.

He said
he was just
lucky
to have been

by himself
up there
in the canyon
after a rain.

He said
it was the
quietest place
he'd ever been
and he stayed there
long enough to
understand
the quiet.

I said,
"I bet you were
surprised
when you heard
those seeds."

But
he said,
"No,
I wasn't surprised at all.
It seemed like the most
natural
thing
in the world."

He just smiled,
remembering.

Byrd Baylor

139

# WRITING activity

## SUMMARY PARAGRAPH

**Prewrite**

In "The Conversation Club" you learned how important listening is. Think about the many ways you used listening today.

Pretend you are a member of the Conversation Club. This is your week to present a subject. Your subject will be the importance of listening. You must present a short opening paragraph on your subject to open the meeting. This paragraph will tell all the ways you used listening in one day.

To collect information for your paragraph, you keep a listening log for one day. In this log, you record all the different ways you used listening. Here is an example of part of a listening log:

---

MY LISTENING LOG FOR _____ (Date) _____

7:00 A.M.  Clock radio woke me up. Listened to the weather; Heard rain on the window

9:00 A.M.  Presented a play in reading class; Had to listen to know when to say my part

4:00 P.M.  Coach gave new rules for the swim team

7:30 P.M.  Conversation with Dad on math homework

---

Remember to record in your log all the ways you used listening for your whole day from morning to evening.

**Write**

Since you will be presenting a short paragraph, you won't be able to use all the information in your log. You will write a summary. A summary gives just the most important ideas about a subject. Here is one way to write your summary. You may think of another.

1. Write a main idea sentence for your paragraph that tells about your subject.
2. Count and report the number of ways you used listening in the morning, afternoon, and evening.
3. Write sentences about one or two interesting examples from your log for each part of the day.
4. Try to use Vocabulary Treasures in your paragraph.
5. Now write the first draft of your paragraph.

> **Vocabulary Treasures**
> astonished    daily
> activities    subject

**Revise**

Read your paragraph. Have a friend read it too. Think about this checklist as you revise.

1. Will your listeners know your main idea? Did you write a clear main idea sentence?
2. Did you give just a few examples from your log?
3. Do all your sentences start with the same words? How could you change some of them?
4. Check the end punctuation in your sentences.
5. Now rewrite your paragraph to share.

# Chin Chiang and the Dragon's Dance

Ian Wallace

Peter Fieldmouse and his new friends shared what they knew by talking and listening. You can also pass on what you know by showing someone how to do something. In this story, a boy named Chin Chiang is taught a special dance—the very old dragon's dance. It is an important part of the Chinese New Year's Day parade held in Chin Chiang's neighborhood every year.

From the time Chin Chiang stood only as high as his grandfather's knees, he had dreamed of dancing the dragon's dance. Now the first day of the Year of the Dragon had arrived and his dream was to come true. Tonight he would dance with his grandfather. But instead of being excited, Chin Chiang was so scared he wanted to melt into his shoes. He knew he could never dance well enough to make Grandfather proud of him.

He stopped sweeping the floor of his family's shop and looked into the street where his mother and father were busy with other shopkeepers. They were hanging up paper lanterns shaped like animals, fish, and birds.

"It's time to practice our parts in the dragon's dance for the last time before the other dancers arrive, Chin Chiang. The afternoon is almost over," called Grandfather Wu from the bakeroom behind the shop.

"If I were a rabbit, I could run far away from here," Chin Chiang said to himself. "But then Mama, Papa, and Grandfather really would be ashamed of me." So very slowly he walked into the bakeroom where Grandfather Wu stood waiting. He was wearing the splendid dragon's head that he would put on again that night for the parade.

"Pick up the silk tail on the floor behind me," said his grandfather from inside the dragon's head. "Together we will be the most magnificent dragon that anyone has ever seen."

Chin Chiang did as he was asked, but as his grandfather started to dance, Chin Chiang did not move. "Grandfather can hide under the dragon's head," he whispered. "But if I trip or fall, I have nowhere to hide. Everyone will say, 'There goes clumsy Chin Chiang.'"

Grandfather Wu stopped dancing. "A dragon must have a tail as well as a head," he said gently.

Chin Chiang looked down at his shoes. "I can't dance the dragon's dance," he said.

"You have trained for a long time, Chin Chiang. Tonight, when you dance, you will bring tears of pride to your parents' eyes. Now come, join me and practice just as we have practiced before."

But when Chin Chiang tried to leap he tripped, stumbled, and fell. Why had he ever thought he could dance the dragon's dance? Why had he ever wanted to? He was much too clumsy.

He jumped up and ran—away from his grandfather, out of the shop, into the market street. He stopped long enough to pick up a rabbit lantern, poke two holes for eyes and shove it over his head.

"Look, look. It's the dragon's tail!" called Mrs. Lau, dangling a speckled salmon for Chin Chiang to see. "Tonight, when you dance, the Great Dragon who lives in the clouds above the mountains will be honored, and next year he will fill our nets with beautiful fish like this."

Chin Chiang turned away.

"And he will grow oranges of a size and color never seen before," called Mr. Koo.

"What they say is true," added Mr. Sing. "The Great Dragon will bring prosperity and good fortune, if your dance pleases him."

But Chin Chiang remembered what one of the other dancers had once told him. If the dance was clumsy, the Great Dragon would be angry. Then he might toss the fruit from the trees and flood the valley. *It will all be my fault,* thought Chin Chiang. *Grandfather Wu will have to choose someone else to dance with him.* He waited to hear no more and raced across the market street.

"Our fish!" called Mrs. Lau.
"Our oranges!" called Mr. Koo.
Chin Chiang turned the corner.

"Our dance," called Grandfather Wu, from the doorway.

Looking out through the lantern, Chin Chiang hurried along the road by the sea to the public library. He had visited it many times when he wanted to be alone. He opened the door and ran up the stairs, round and round, higher and higher, up, up, up, to the door at the top that led out to the roof.

From his perch in the sky he could see the mountains rising above the sea. Below him were the animal lanterns, which would glow like tiny stars tonight. Chin Chiang felt happier than he had for many days.

"I never expected to meet a rabbit on top of this roof," called a strange voice.

Chin Chiang turned around quickly. A woman carrying a mop and pail was coming toward him.

"I'm not a rabbit," he said shyly. "I am Chin Chiang," and he pulled off the lantern.

"Oh, that is much better," she said. "Greetings, Chin Chiang. My name is Pu Yee. May I enjoy the view with you?" She didn't wait for a reply. "In a little while I'll be watching the New Year's parade from here.

I used to dance the dragon's dance when I was young, but not any more. My feet are too old."

"My grandfather dances the dragon's dance," said Chin Chiang, "and his feet are as old as yours."

Pu Yee laughed. "His old shoes may move his old bones, but my feet will never dance again."

A wonderful idea suddenly came to Chin Chiang. What if he had found someone to dance in his place? He would show Pu Yee his part in the dance right now. No one could see them if they tripped or fell. "You can help me practice what my grandfather taught me," he said.

"Oh, my creaky bones, what a funny sight that will be," said Pu Yee.

"You can dance," he told her. Cautiously Chin Chiang gave a little jump. Pu Yee jumped too. He shook slowly at first and she shook too. Next they leaped into the air, landed together, and spun on their heels. Before long Pu Yee had forgotten her creaky bones. Then Chin Chiang stumbled and fell.

"Let's try again," said Pu Yee, picking him up.

While they danced, darkness had crept down slowly from the mountains to the city below. Then, from far off, Chin Chiang heard the tune of pigeons with whistles tied to their tail feathers. They had been set free from their cages in the marketplace and were flying high above the buildings. Chin Chiang knew this meant the New Year Festival had begun.

"We must go, Pu Yee. We're late," said Chin Chiang. "The pigeons are flying free."

"*I'm* not late," she replied. "I'm staying here."

But Chin Chiang pulled her by the hand, and they hurried down the stairs together— round and round, down, down, down, to the market street. Chin Chang pushed his way forward, but Pu Yee pulled back. In the noise and confusion Chin Chiang let go of her hand, and suddenly he came face to face with the dragon whose head was circled in smoke.

"Where have you been, Chin Chiang? I have been sick with worry," called Grandfather Wu in a muffled voice. Chin Chiang did not reply. "Come now, take up the tail before the smoke disappears and everyone can see us."

Chin Chiang stood still, his feet frozen to the ground. "I can't dance, Grandfather," he said.

Grandfather Wu turned away. "You can dance, Chin Chiang. Follow me."

"Look, look. Here comes the dragon!" called Mr. Sing. The crowd sent up a cheer that bounced off windows and doors and jumped into the sky.

Chin Chiang was trapped. Slowly he stooped and picked up the tail. Grandfather Wu shook the dragon's head fiercely until Chin Chiang started to kick up his heels to the beat of the thundering drum.

Then, suddenly, Chin Chiang stumbled, but instead of falling he did a quick step and recovered his balance. Excitedly, he leaped into the air, and again, and higher again. As the dance went on, Chin Chiang's feet moved more surely, his steps grew firmer, and his leaps more daring. Mrs. Lau and Mr. Koo cheered from their market shops while people poured out of their houses onto balconies and sidewalks, filling the streets.

Just then Chin Chiang caught sight of a familiar face in the crowd. It was Pu Yee. Chin Chiang leaped to the sidewalk and pulled her into the street.

"I can't, Chin Chiang," she said, pulling away. "My bones. My bones. My knees."

"Pu Yee, yes, you can," Chin Chiang said. "Look at me!" Hesitantly she took hold of the tail and together they kicked up their heels just as they had on the rooftop, while people cheered them on. Up one street and down another they danced, to the beat of the thundering drum.

All too soon the dragon lifted its head and shook its tail for the last time. The dance was over. Pu Yee hugged Chin Chiang close.

Grandfather Wu smiled inside the dragon's head. "Bring your new friend to our home for dinner, Chin Chiang," he said. Pu Yee and Chin Chiang hopped quickly over the doorstep and into the bakeshop.

The family exchanged gifts of fine teas in wooden boxes, new clothes, and small red envelopes of Lucky Money. Then they sat together to share plates of meat dumplings and carp, bowls of steaming soup, and trays of delicious cakes and fresh fruit.

"To Chin Chiang, the very best dragon's tail I have ever seen," said Grandfather Wu, raising his glass in a toast.

Chin Chiang's face glowed with pride. "To a prosperous Year of the Dragon," he said, raising his glass to his mama, papa, grandfather, and his new friend Pu Yee.

## Questions

1. Why didn't Chin Chiang want to do the dragon's dance?

2. How did Chin Chiang and Pu Yee help each other?

3. Why do you think it was important for Chin Chiang to dance the dragon's dance?

4. If you had the chance to be in a parade, what would you be?

## Applying Reading Skills
### Realism and Fantasy

"Chin Chiang and the Dragon's Dance" is about a boy and a dragon, but it is a realistic story. Write the sentences that describe events that really happened.

The people in the street slowly formed one large dragon.

Chin Chiang stood with his feet frozen to the ground.

The paper lanterns in the shop suddenly turned into animals, fish, and birds.

Chin Chiang became a rabbit and ran away as fast as he could.

Grandfather smiled inside the dragon's head.

# PEOPLE

—Charlotte Zolotow—

Some people talk and talk
and never say a thing.
Some people look at you
and birds begin to sing.

Some people laugh and laugh
and yet you want to cry.
Some people touch your hand
and music fills the sky.

156

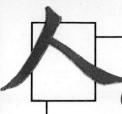

# CHINESE PICTURE WORDS

The Chinese language is written in a different way than English. In English, we use an alphabet to spell words. The Chinese use pictures to make their words.

The Chinese word for *tree* is

What do you think this word is?
It is the word for forest.

This is the word for *man*.
Can you see the two legs?

This is the word for *woman*.
It has two legs, too.

This is how the Chinese write *horse*.
Can you see the four legs and the tail?

You can make your own kind of picture language. Choose a picture to mean *rode*. Then write a picture sentence that says: *The man rode the horse in the forest.*

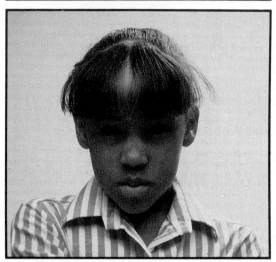
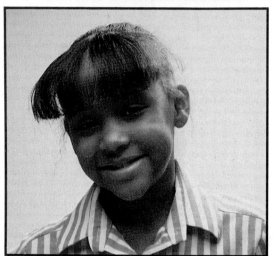

# COMMUNICATION

*Valerie Pitt*

You have read about people and animals communicating in different ways.

Communication helps us to learn a lot about things and about each other. This article tells about the many ways we have of sharing information, thoughts, and feelings.

What do you wish for more than anything in the world? A puppy of your own? A new baseball bat? Maybe you have told your family and your best friends exactly what it is you want most. By talking to them you have *shared* this information.

Suppose that on your birthday you are given a puppy of your own. It has soft ears and big eyes. It is so happy to see you that it licks your face all over. To show the puppy how pleased you are to have it, you hug it. You pat its soft ears. You are so happy that you smile—a great big smile. Through your smile, words, and actions you have *shared* your happiness with your family and your new puppy.

That is what communication is all about. Communication means sharing information, thoughts, and feelings.

We communicate all the time. We do it every day of our lives. Most of the time we communicate by talking. We put our thoughts and ideas into words. Other people understand and use these same words. Think of all the millions of words that are spoken in your town or city alone. Think how many are spoken in one day in your home. How many are spoken in offices, in stores, and in restaurants? Think about your classroom and on the streets. Words, words, words. Everyone has ideas and information to share.

But sometimes it takes too long to share information with a lot of words. That is why we have signs and symbols. They tell a lot of people the same things at the same time. The sound of an ambulance bell tells you that someone has been hurt. It says get out of the way quickly. Red traffic lights tell you to STOP! Traffic is moving in another direction. Signs on doors tell you to PULL or PUSH. Others tell where to go in and out.

People can also communicate with one another quickly without saying a word. Just by raising your hand, you can let your teacher know that you want to say something. You may want to ask or answer a question. By putting your finger to your lips, you can tell someone to be quiet. By waving your arm, you can signal a friendly "hello" to someone.

Feelings are sometimes hard to put into words. People often communicate their feelings by the look on their faces. You can smile . . . frown . . . laugh. You can show anger or fear, happiness or surprise. There is a whole theater in your face and in all the faces around you.

The way people sit and walk and use their hands tells about their feelings, too. If you are bored, you may slump in a chair or drum your fingers on the table. If you are excited about a birthday party, you may rush around smiling at everyone. If you are in a bad mood, you may kick a stone or glare at everybody.

 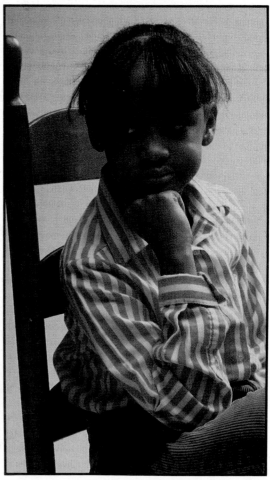

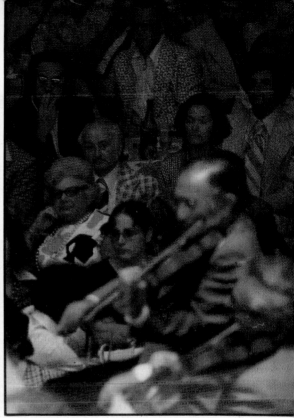

People can communicate through the things they create. An artist can communicate many different things in his or her paintings. One of the paintings can tell about summer. It can tell how cool it feels to lie under the trees. Other paintings can tell other things.

A composer can communicate many ideas and feelings through music. One piece of music may sound like waves crashing against the shore. Another may sound like soldiers marching to battle. Music can make a listener feel happy or sad. It can make you ready to rush off and do great things.

Authors can write books to tell about all the wonderful things in the world. In their books, authors can also tell about people and their feelings. Books can show us that we all feel the same things. It does not matter who we are or where we live.

Things like paintings, music, and books help us to communicate with one another. So do magazines, newspapers, television and radio, and movies. We call these things communications. A name for these ways of communicating is communications "media." They help us to find out what is going on in the world and in other people's minds.

When Neil Armstrong made the first step on the moon, people all around the world saw him do it. All those people heard him say: "A small step for man, a giant leap for mankind." Television carried his voice and picture from the moon. Television helps bring the people of the world together. Through television many people are able to see and hear the same thing at the same time. With television, people watch things at the minute they are happening. It is almost instant communication.

Modern communications help us to find out things quickly. We can share thoughts with other people very quickly, too. We can pick up a telephone and speak to someone in almost any country in the world. On a ship at sea we can talk to other ships by radio telephone. We can record programs on videotape. We can receive and exchange large amounts of information by computer.

Communications help us to learn about the present, the past, and the future. All kinds of exciting new ways of communicating will be developed in the future. Space stations, laser beams maybe something no one has even thought of yet lie in our future.

## Questions

1. What are two ways people communicate without using words?

2. How might a painter make a painting look cool? How might a composer make his or her music sound like soldiers marching?

3. How would your life be different without modern communications?

4. If you were an inventor, what new method of communication would you develop?

## Applying Reading Skills
### Follow Directions

One way to communicate is to give directions. Try to communicate with someone using these directions.

> Draw an arrow pointing to the left.
>
> Draw a square to the right of the arrow.
>
> Write *Don't Walk* in the square.

Now write your own set of directions in three steps.

# *One to Another*

The stories you read in *One to Another* told about communication among people. When one of the story characters wanted to express a thought or idea, he or she had to think of a way to do it. The communicator could use either words, actions, or symbols. Which characters were able to get their messages across clearly?

## Thinking About *One to Another*

1. Tell how miscommunication confused the boy in "Gila Monsters Meet You at the Airport," the man in "The Great Minu," and the animals in "Why Mosquitoes Buzz in People's Ears."

2. What were Maxie in "Maxie" and Peter Fieldmouse in "The Conversation Club" trying to tell their friends?

3. Which stories could have really happened? Why do you think so?

4. Why do you think *One to Another* is a good name for this unit? Use examples from the stories in your answer.

5. Write about three ways you communicated to people yesterday without words. Did they understand your message?

# Introducing Level 8
# Unit 2
# On the Move

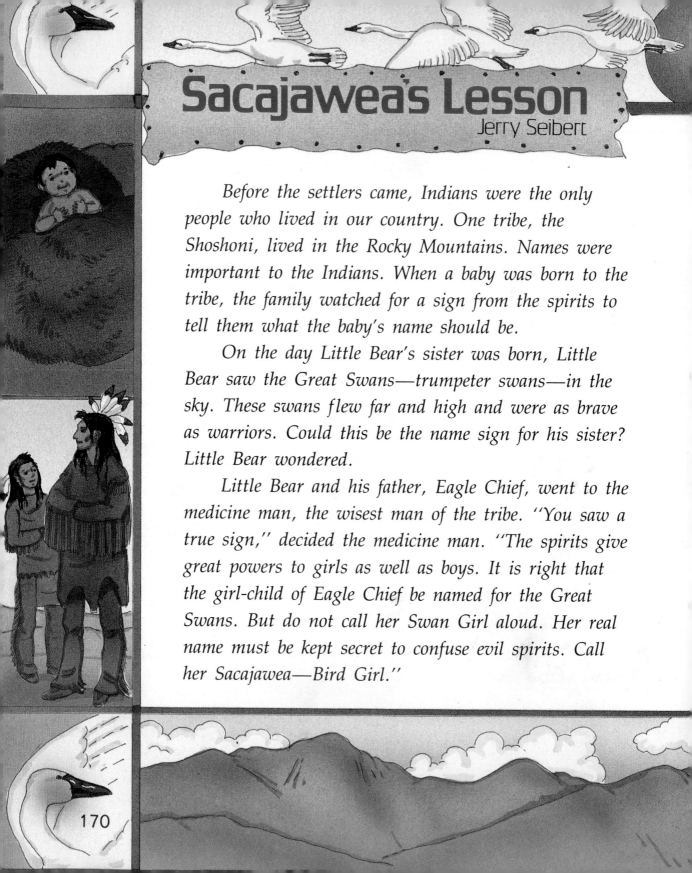

# Sacajawea's Lesson

Jerry Seibert

Before the settlers came, Indians were the only people who lived in our country. One tribe, the Shoshoni, lived in the Rocky Mountains. Names were important to the Indians. When a baby was born to the tribe, the family watched for a sign from the spirits to tell them what the baby's name should be.

On the day Little Bear's sister was born, Little Bear saw the Great Swans—trumpeter swans—in the sky. These swans flew far and high and were as brave as warriors. Could this be the name sign for his sister? Little Bear wondered.

Little Bear and his father, Eagle Chief, went to the medicine man, the wisest man of the tribe. "You saw a true sign," decided the medicine man. "The spirits give great powers to girls as well as boys. It is right that the girl-child of Eagle Chief be named for the Great Swans. But do not call her Swan Girl aloud. Her real name must be kept secret to confuse evil spirits. Call her Sacajawea—Bird Girl."

Little Bear remembered the words of the medicine man. Sacajawea might need to know many things other girls did not. Who could teach her better than her big brother?

He taught her to swim as the braves did. She learned to slip through the icy mountain streams with hardly a ripple, and to swim with a heavy pack on her back.

One of the most important lessons a brave learned was to be able to tell always exactly where he was by day or night. It was a disgrace for a warrior to be lost even though he had traveled for many suns.

Little Bear taught Sacajawea to find her way through the trackless forest and narrow mountain passes.

"Watch carefully as you travel," he said. "Remember landmarks—big things like the curve of a peak against the sky, and small things like the crooked branch of a tree."

"You are wasting your time," said the other boys. "A girl can't learn the lessons of a brave."

"Sacajawea can," said Little Bear. One day she proved it. They were a long way from home. Sacajawea had never been in this part of the mountains before. Little Bear saw an eagle's nest high on a cliff.

"Let us see if there are eaglets in the nest," he said.

"Eagles used to be Shoshoni people," he told Sacajawea as they climbed the steep cliff. "The spirits gave them strong magic so they could turn themselves into eagles. They flew high and far to watch for enemies. Then an evil spirit, from another tribe, stole the magic that turned them back into people. Eagles are still Shoshoni. But without the magic they can't become people again."

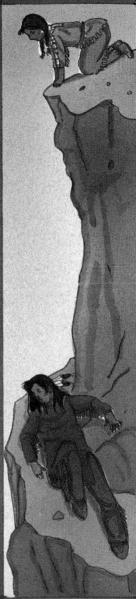

It was hard to find footholds on the steep cliff. As Little Bear climbed along a sharp rock, there was a sudden cracking sound. The rock went crashing down the mountain.

Sacajawea looked down fearfully. She could see nothing but gray rocks. Suddenly she heard Little Bear's voice. For a minute she wondered if he were a spirit. Then she saw him lying on a narrow ledge part way down the cliff. All around him the sides of the cliff were straight up and down.

"You must go for help," he called. "There is no way for me to climb off this ledge."

Sacajawea worked her way back down the cliff slowly and carefully. The sun had set when she reached the valley. She stopped to study the landmarks carefully while there was still some light. Then she started off at a quick, steady trot. She wanted to run but she knew she would tire much faster if she ran.

It grew dark. The stars began their march across the sky. The moon floated above the peaks. Sacajawea had never been alone in the forest at night before. It seemed very quiet. The smallest noise seemed very loud.

The mountains made shadows in the moonlight. Sacajawea stopped often to note the black and silver outlines that looked so different in the daytime.

Black clouds rolled across the sky and hid the moon and stars. It began to rain. Even the dark shapes of the mountains were blotted out.

Sacajawea curled up under a tree. The cold rain dripped through the leaves. Close by, something crashed through the trees. Was it an elk—or a white bear (grizzly)? Her heart pounded. Even the bravest warriors were afraid of white bears.

Then she thought of Little Bear lying on the narrow ledge.

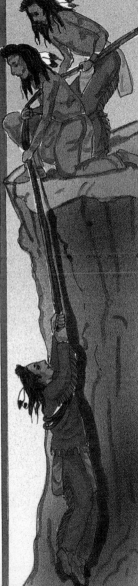

"Little Bear is depending on me," she told herself.

As soon as the first light came in the east she started on. The sun was still high in the sky when she reached the village.

"I know the place," said Eagle Chief when she told him what had happened. "Eagles have always nested there."

He set off at once with a party of braves. They carried long rawhide ropes and rode their fastest horses. The next day Little Bear was home with only a few cuts and bruises to show for his fall.

"You traveled swiftly, Little Sister," he told Sacajawea. "It was a hard trail through strange country. No brave could have done better."

Sacajawea knew he could give her no higher praise.

The story you just read was about a real girl. Sacajawea lived up to her name and grew up to become a famous guide. When Meriwether Lewis and William Clark were sent by President Jefferson in 1804 to explore the West, they met Sacajawea along the way. She guided Lewis and Clark through lands she knew from her childhood. A river, a peak, and a mountain pass have been named after her.

WESTWARD THE STAR OF EMPIRE TAKES ITS WAY

## Questions

1. What did Little Bear teach Sacajawea?

2. Why did Little Bear fall?

3. Why do you think Sacajawea studied the landmarks carefully on her way to get help?

4. Think about the route you travel from home to school. What are some of the landmarks along the way?

### Applying Reading Skills
### Main Idea

Read the following paragraph about Sacajawea. Then copy the paragraph and draw a line under the main idea. Draw two lines under the supporting details.

Sacajawea learned to swim swiftly and well. She learned to slip through the icy mountain streams with hardly a ripple. She could even swim with a heavy pack on her back.

# I GO FORTH TO MOVE
# ABOUT THE EARTH

I go forth to move about the earth.
I go forth as the owl, wise and knowing.
I go forth as the eagle, powerful and bold.
I go forth as the dove, powerful and gentle.
I go forth to move about the earth
  in wisdom, courage, and peace.

Alonzo Lopez
Papago Indian

# SKILLS activity

## SUMMARIZE

When you **summarize** sentences, you tell what they say in a shorter way. You can summarize many sentences in one sentence. Your summary should tell the most important information. Summarizing can help you remember important information you read.

**ACTIVITY A**   Read the sentences below. Then choose the sentence that best summarizes what they say. Write the sentence on your paper.

One of the most important lessons an Indian brave learned was to be able to tell exactly where he was by day or night. It was a disgrace for a warrior to be lost even though he had travelled for many suns.

a. To avoid disgrace, a brave learned to know where he was at all times.
b. A brave learned to travel for many suns.

Black clouds rolled across the sky and hid the setting sun. It began to rain. Even the dark shapes of the mountains were blotted out.

a. The sky turned black and it began to rain.
b. It was hard to see the mountains.

**ACTIVITY B** Read each group of sentences below. Then write a sentence that best summarizes what each group says. Use your own words in your summary sentence. Write your sentence on your paper.

On the day Little Bear's sister was born, Little Bear saw the Great Swans in the sky. These swans flew far and high and were as brave as warriors. Could this be the name sign for his sister?

He taught her to swim as the braves did. She learned to slip through the icy mountain streams with hardly a ripple and to swim with a heavy pack on her back.

It grew dark. The moon floated above the peaks. Sacajawea had never been alone in the forest before. It seemed very quiet.

# THE COURAGE OF SARAH NOBLE

**Alice Dalgliesh**

*Like Sacajawea, the new settlers of America had to be brave as they traveled through strange country. In this story, you will meet another real girl who lived long ago. In 1707, Sarah Noble went with her father to build a new home in Connecticut. Sarah had many adventures, and sometimes she was frightened. But she always remembered what her mother told her:* **Keep up your courage, Sarah Noble.**

Sarah lay on a quilt under a tree. The darkness was all around her, but through the branches she could see one bright star. It was comfortable to look at.

The spring night was cold, and Sarah drew her warm cloak close. That was comfortable, too. She thought of how her mother had put it around her the day she and her father started out on this long, hard journey.

"Keep up your courage," her mother had said, fastening the cloak under Sarah's chin. "Keep up your courage, Sarah Noble!"

And, indeed, Sarah needed to keep up her courage, for she and her father had been traveling all the way into the wilderness of Connecticut.

Although their journey was almost over, this was the first night they had spent in the forest. The other nights they had come to a settlement. Thomas, the brown horse, was tied nearby. He was asleep on his feet. Against a tree Sarah's father sat, his musket across his knees. Sometimes he nodded, but Sarah knew that if she called to him he would wake. Suddenly she had a great need to hear his voice, even though she could not see his face.

"Wooo—oooh!" Such a strange sound from a nearby tree.

"Father?"

"An owl, Sarah. He is telling you goodnight."

Another longer, louder sound, a stranger sound, as if someone were in pain.

"Father?"

"A fox, Sarah. He is no bigger than a dog.
He is calling to his mate."

Sarah closed her eyes and tried to sleep.
Then came a sound that made her open her eyes
and sit right up.

"FATHER!"

"Yes, Sarah, it is a wolf. But I have my
musket, and I am awake."

"I can't sleep, Father. Tell me about home."

"What shall I tell you, Sarah?"

"Anything—if it is about home."

*Now the howl of the wolf was a little farther
away.*

"You remember how it was, Sarah, the day I
came home to tell of the land I had bought? You
were rocking the baby in the cradle . . ."

"And the baby would not sleep."

"And your mother said . . ."

"You know I cannot take the baby on a long journey. She is so young and she is not strong."

*The wolf was farther away, but still one could hear it.*

"And you said . . ."

"I said, 'I will go and cook for you, Father.'"

But she felt suddenly and terribly lonely for her mother and for the big family of brothers and sisters. John . . . David . . . Stephen . . . Mary . . . Hannah . . . three-year-old Margaret . . . the baby . . . . And—*could* she really cook? She had never made a pie. But—maybe—you—don't—need—pies—in—the—wilderness. Keep—up—your—courage—Sarah—Noble. Keep—up . . . . And holding tightly to a fold of the warm cloak, Sarah was asleep.

Now the wolf was very far away. But
Thomas, who had raised his head when he heard
it, still stood with his ears lifted . . . listening.

And Sarah's father sat there, wondering
if he should have brought this child into the
wilderness. When the first light of morning came
through the trees, he was still awake.

The next night was quite different. After a
long journey they came to a settlement, and a
family took Sarah and her father into their home.
Sarah lay on her quilt by the fire, but the house
was so strange to her that she was not comforted
by its warmth. Sarah held her cloak close and
whispered to herself, "Keep up your courage,
Sarah Noble." But it was quite a long time before
she slept.

Now they had come to the last day of the journey. The Indian trail had been narrow, the hills went up and down, up and down. Sarah and her father were tired, and even Thomas walked wearily.

By late afternoon they would be home. Home? No, it wasn't really home, just a place out in the wilderness. But after a while it would be home. John Noble told Sarah it would be. His voice kept leading her on.

"Now we must be about two miles away."

"Now it is surely a mile . . . only a mile."

Sarah's tired feet seemed to dance. She picked some wild flowers and stuck them into the harness behind Thomas's ear.

"You must be well dressed, Thomas," she said. "We are coming home."

She put a pink flower on her own dress and her feet danced along again. Then suddenly she stopped.

"Father, if there is no house where shall we live?"

Her father smiled down at her. "I have told you . . ."

"Then tell me again. I like to hear."

"I hope to find a cave in the side of a hill," he said. "I will make a hut for us, and a fence around it. Then you and Thomas and I will live there until the house is built."

Now they had come to the top of a long, steep hill and they stopped at a place where there were not many trees, only bushes and coarse grass.

"This is one of the bare places," John Noble said. "The Indians have cleared it for a hunting ground."

Behind the bushes something stirred . . . . Sarah looked around her fearfully.

"A deer," said her father, and raised his gun. But Sarah clung to him.

"No, Father, no! Do not shoot it!"

"But we must have meat."

"Not now, not now," Sarah begged. "Its eyes are so gentle, Father."

"Well . . ." said John Noble. But he did not shoot. The deer rushed away, its white tail showing like a flag. Then Sarah drew a long breath and looked down.

Below there was a valley. "And you would see the Great River if it were not for the trees," her father said.

Sarah looked and looked and filled her mind with the beauty of it. It was a beauty that would stay with her all her life. Beyond the valley there were green hills, and beyond . . . and beyond . . . and beyond . . . more hills of a strange, soft and misty blue.

The trees were the dark green of firs and the light green of birches in springtime. And now they were friendly. They were not like the angry dark trees that had seemed to stand in their path as they came.

Now Sarah held her courage a little more firmly. She also held tightly to her father's hand. And so they came, with Thomas, down the long hill into the place that would be their home.

*Sarah faced many tests of courage in the days and weeks to come. You can find out more about her adventures by reading the rest of* **The Courage of Sarah Noble.**

# Questions

1. What did Sarah's mother say to Sarah before the journey?

2. Why was Sarah afraid the night she and her father spent in the forest?

3. When do you think Sarah's mother and the rest of the family will join Sarah and her father?

4. Suppose you were a settler picking a place to build a new home. Write a paragraph describing the place you would pick.

## Applying Reading Skills
### Predict Outcomes

Use complete sentences to answer the questions about "The Courage of Sarah Noble."

1. What do you think Sarah and her father did when they got to the place that would be their home?

2. Do you think Sarah kept her courage in the days and weeks to come? Why or why not?

3. How do you know that Sarah will probably grow to like her new home?

# Alice Dalgliesh

Alice Dalgliesh was born in the British West Indies. Growing up, she lived in a very close-knit family. Dalgliesh was allowed to read anything in her parents' large library. Both her parents and teachers read aloud often.

As a young adult, Dalgliesh came to America, studied education, and became a teacher. Later she was a book editor.

Dalgliesh had begun writing stories when she was six, and continued to write them throughout her life. As a teacher and editor, she knew what children liked to read. Dalgliesh felt that children enjoyed stories about the things they knew, books that could be read aloud over and over, and books that were sometimes funny. Do you think that Alice Dalgliesh's books have met her own test for what makes a good book?

**More to Read**     *The Thanksgiving Story*
*The Bears on Hemlock Mountain*

# A Birthday for General Washington

## Johanna Johnston

When Sarah Noble and her father built their new
home, Connecticut was an English colony. A colony is
an area of land that is under the control of another
country. By 1763, England had thirteen colonies in
America, along the Atlantic coast. Some of the colonists
wanted to break away from England. On July 4, 1776,
the colonists declared their freedom, or independence.
But to gain independence they had to fight a long war.

George Washington led the soldiers in the War for
Independence. But it took the bravery of many people
for America to finally become an independent nation.
This play tells about how the courage of two children
helped the American cause and turned February 22,
1778, into George Washington's happiest birthday.

### Characters:

Narrators

George Washington

A Lieutenant

Martha Washington

A Corporal

Miller Goodman

Mistress Goodman

Jonathan Goodman

Abigail Goodman

Four Continental Soldiers

# PROLOGUE

*(The narrators, two Continental soldiers, enter in front of the curtain.)*

**First Soldier:**  It was the winter of 1778. Americans had been fighting for independence from England for almost three years.

**Second Soldier:**  With George Washington as our commander-in-chief we had won some victories. But then came a time of defeat.

**First Soldier:**  The English captured New York City—then Philadelphia.

**Second Soldier:**  Then cold weather came and General Washington led us to winter quarters on a lonely stretch of land called Valley Forge, some miles beyond Philadelphia.

**First Soldier:**  We cut down trees to build huts. We went looking for food.

**Second Soldier:**  But the supplies we were counting on from the Continental Congress and the different states did not come.

**First Soldier:**  We had no blankets against the cold. Our clothes were in rags, our shoes worn out. Worst of all, we did not have enough food.

**Second Soldier:**  Let us take you back to that time—to the farmhouse near the camp where General Washington had his headquarters.

## ACT I

Headquarters of General George Washington
Valley Forge, 1778

### ★ CURTAIN RISES ★

**Washington:** Just a minute, Lieutenant. As soon as I seal this letter it will be ready.

**Lieutenant:** I will ride with it at once, sir. I will deliver it to Congress without delay.

**Washington:** I know you will use all speed. If only Congress would answer as quickly.

**Lieutenant:** Sir, sometimes I wonder. Is it possible that the Congress is losing faith in the cause of independence?

**Washington:** No, no, do not say so, Lieutenant! It has been a hard winter for the members of Congress also. They had to flee to York when the British took Philadelphia. Some of them have been ill.

**Lieutenant:** Still, they are quartered in warm houses. Their clothes are not in rags. They have shoes. They have *food*.

**Washington:** Yes, I know, Lieutenant.

**Lieutenant:** You write letter after letter, sir, telling them of our hardships here, but week after week goes by and we get no supplies.

*(There is a knock at the door.)*

**Washington:** Come in.

*(Enter Martha Washington.)*

**Martha:** Good afternoon, George. Good afternoon, Lieutenant.

**Washington:** Martha, do come in. The lieutenant is just leaving.

**Lieutenant:** Good afternoon, ma'am. I will be on my way, sir.

**Washington:** Very good.

*(Exit Lieutenant.)*

**Washington:** What can I do for you, Martha?

**Martha:** I would like it if you left that desk for half an hour and came to have a bite to eat with me.

**Washington:** I'm sorry, Martha. I still have many letters to write. I must write again to Governor Trumbull of Connecticut. He, at least, has always been helpful.

**Martha:**   George, I traveled here from Mount Vernon to see that you do not wear yourself out from work. You *must* rest now and then. Besides—have you forgotten? Today is your birthday.

**Washington:**   My birthday! I think I would rather forget it, Martha. Half of the soldiers are walking barefoot in the snow. They will have nothing to eat tonight but cornmeal bread—johnnycake—no meat at all. It does not seem a day to celebrate.

*(There is a knock on the door.)*

**Washington:**   Come in.

*(Enter Corporal.)*

**Washington:**   Yes, Corporal. What is it?

**Corporal:**   Bad news, sir. The wagonload of cornmeal we were expecting from Goodman, the miller over on the east branch, has not arrived as promised. The men will not even have johnnycake for supper tonight.

**Martha:**   Not even johnnycake!

**Corporal:**   No, ma'am.

**Washington:**   You see, Martha! It is not a day to celebrate. I cannot remember a day when things looked worse for the American cause.

★ **CURTAIN** ★

# ACT II
## Goodman's Mill, near Valley Forge

*(The two narrators enter and take their places before the curtain.)*

**First Soldier:** A few miles away from Valley Forge is Goodman's mill. Outside, the mill wheel turns slowly in the icy stream. A horse waits patiently by a wagon.

**Second Soldier:** But inside the house the miller lies in pain. His wife, his son, and his daughter are trying to comfort him.

## ★ CURTAIN RISES ★

**Jonathan:** Please, Mother. I want to do something to help General Washington.

**Abigail:** I do, too. Oh, I can't bear to think that he is hungry and cold.

**Jonathan:** Let us go, Father!

**Miller Goodman:** You really think you can find the way?

**Jonathan:** Oh yes—yes! Come, Abigail, let's get started.

**Abigail:** Just one minute, Brother. There is something I have to take with me.

*(Exit Abigail.)*

**Mistress Goodman:** But at least you must bundle up well.

*(Enter Abigail. She wears a cape underneath which she is hiding something.)*

**Abigail:** All right, Jonathan, I'm ready.

**Jonathan:** I'm ready, too. Don't worry. We'll get the cornmeal to the General.

★ **CURTAIN** ★

## ACT III
### General Washington's Headquarters

### ★ CURTAIN RISES ★

*(Later that same afternoon.)*

**Martha:** I have never seen you so discouraged.

**Washington:** I do not know how much longer the men can endure their hardships, Martha.

**Martha:** You fear they will begin to desert.

**Washington:** Who could blame them? They have suffered for months! But what hurts me most is that our own countrymen do not care enough even to see that our soldiers have food to eat.

*(There is a knock on the door.)*

**Washington:** Come in.

*(Enter Corporal.)*

**Corporal:** Sir, good news.

**Washington:** *(eagerly)* Yes? What kind of news?

**Corporal:** The cornmeal arrived after all, sir. The men will eat tonight.

**Martha:** Oh, I am so glad!

**Washington:** Thank goodness! Not all our countrymen have forgotten us.

**Corporal:** Perhaps, sir, you might like to meet the wagon driver and his assistant?

**Washington:**   Certainly. Bring them in.

*(Corporal goes to the door, signals to Abigail and Jonathan who enter.)*

**Corporal:**   Abigail and Jonathan Goodman, sir and ma'am.

**Martha:**   Why, they are just children!

**Washington:**   You two alone brought the cornmeal?

**Jonathan:**   Sir, our father hurt his back so badly he could not come. But he knew how great was your need.

**Abigail:**   He told us that you were cold, too. So I brought you this. I knitted it myself.

*(She takes a long woolen scarf from under her cape.)*

203

**Washington:** How can I thank you? How can I thank you both? You cannot know what it means to me to learn that America still has patriots—and young ones, too—our hope for the future. All at once, I again have hope for the American cause.

**Corporal:** Sir, a group of soldiers are outside and wish to speak to you.

**Washington:** Let them in.

*(Corporal ushers in four ragged soldiers.)*

**First Soldier:** Sir, we have come with a special message from all the troops.

**Second Soldier:** We want you to know that we will stand by you and our cause.

**Third Soldier:** Winter will not last forever. Better times will come.

**Fourth Soldier:** We especially wanted to tell you so today, because we have another message for you. All together now!

**All Soldiers:** Happy birthday, General Washington! Happy birthday to you!

**Abigail:** Oh, is it your birthday, sir?

**Jonathan:** Really?

**Martha:** Yes, it is his birthday. A little while ago he thought it was a sad day.

**Washington:** But now I'm beginning to think it is the happiest birthday of my life—thanks to all of you. Thanks to you, Jonathan and Abigail. Thanks to you men, for giving me new hope and faith—the best birthday presents of all. Shall we celebrate with johnnycake?

★ **CURTAIN** ★

# EPILOGUE

**First Soldier:** Better times *did* come.

**Second Soldier:** Just a few days after the General's birthday word came that France had recognized the United States as a new and independent nation.

**First Soldier:** Even better, the French were sending men and ships to help us fight.

**Second Soldier:** A famous soldier, Baron von Steuben, came from Germany to help train the American troops. Another fine soldier, Thaddeus Kosciosko, came from Poland.

**First Soldier:** Supplies began to arrive at last.

**Second Soldier:** Spring came, and we were ready to fight again.

**First Soldier:** The war did not end soon. But in many ways the General's birthday marked the turn to final victory.

**Second Soldier:** Washington would celebrate many more birthdays, some as first President of the new nation. But none was quite so sad— then glad—as the one on February 22, 1778, at Valley Forge.

### ★ CURTAIN ★

## Questions

1. What supplies did the soldiers at Valley Forge need?

2. Why was General Washington becoming discouraged?

3. What kind of children do you think Abigail and Jonathan were?

4. What qualities do you think a leader should have? Why do you think they are important?

## Applying Reading Skills
### Predict Outcomes

Use complete sentences to answer the questions about "A Birthday for General Washington."

1. How did you know before you were told what Jonathan and Abigail would bring to General Washington?

2. What clues helped you know what Abigail had hidden under her coat?

3. How do you think the men will celebrate Washington's birthday?

208

# WHICH WASHINGTON?

There are many Washingtons:
Which one do you like best?
The rich man with his powdered wig
And silk brocaded vest?

The sportsman from Virginia
Riding with his hounds,
Sounding a silver trumpet
On the green resplendent grounds?

The President with his tricorne hat
And polished leather boots,
With scarlet capes and ruffled shirts
And fine brass-buttoned suits?

Or the patchwork man with ragged feet,
Freezing at Valley Forge,
Richer in courage than all of them—
Though all of them were George.

Eve Merriam

# FELIPE and FILOMENA

## Genevieve Gray

*While the colonists were fighting to gain their independence from England, much of America was still unsettled. Most of the land west of the Mississippi River belonged to Spain and France. In the 1700s, people from Mexico began to settle the land that is now the state of California. This story tells about one such group of settlers.*

Felipe lived with Uncle Carlos, Aunt Maria, and his six cousins. His friend was Filomena, a baby burro. Filomena was very loud but very small—too small to help on the farm.

Uncle Carlos tried to grow corn but the land was poor. Felipe and his cousins were often hungry. So were most people in their town in Mexico.

One day in the plaza, Felipe and Filomena saw an officer talking to the crowd. "I am Colonel Anza," he said. "The Viceroy of Mexico needs thirty families to settle in California. The rich land there is good for farms and ranches."

"Each family will get clothes, food, horses, and ranch animals—all free. California is four months away by horseback. My soldiers and I will take you there. Who will go?"

211

"Food? Clothes?" Felipe whispered to Filomena. Then he shouted, "I will go!" Others began to shout, "We will go to California!"

Filomena cried, EEEEEAW—ee—AW!" She was so loud that horses reared and pigs squealed.

"Get that burro out of here!" cried Colonel Anza.

Felipe ran to tell Uncle Carlos. "California is far away," said Uncle Carlos, "but we need the food and clothes." They went to sign up.

At last everything was ready. Colonel Anza led the caravan. Behind him rode soldiers. Then came the families and more soldiers, then the pack mules and the cattle. At the end came Filomena.

Felipe rode on a horse. He looked and looked for Filomena. Then he heard her calling him. "EEEEEAW—ee—AW—ee—AW!" The horses jerked the reins, the mules threw off their loads, and cattle ran into the bushes.

The caravan stopped. "Get rid of that burro!" shouted Colonel Anza. But no one heard him, because they were too busy catching animals.

Late that afternoon, Colonel Anza stopped beside a stream. "We will camp here for the night," he said. Men unloaded the mules and put up tents. Women built cooking fires and started supper. Children played in the woods.

Felipe found Filomena eating grass with the mules. "I love you, Filomena," whispered Felipe. The burro put her head against his chest.

The next morning a soldier blew a horn
for time-to-get-up. Filomena sang along,
"EEEEEAW—ee—AW—ee—AW!" Everybody got
up very fast. Colonel Anza laughed. "This burro
is not so bad," he said. After that, Filomena sang
"time-to-get-up" every morning. Felipe was
proud. Even Uncle Carlos looked a little pleased.

A few days later they came to a mountain
pass. Rocks rose high all around. Colonel Anza
was afraid of an Indian attack. "Apache scouts
will be watching from those rocks," he said. They
went through the narrow pass. They climbed
through a canyon, and they crept along a ledge.
No one slept that night. All night, Felipe listened
for Apaches. He thought he saw some scouts, but
they were only shadows.

The caravan moved out at dawn. Nobody ate breakfast. "By noon, we will be safe," said Colonel Anza. "Then we will eat."

"California better be good!" grumbled Aunt Maria.

"If we ever get there," said Uncle Carlos.

They rode for weeks through miles and miles and miles of desert. At last they came to a river. Indians lived along the bank. "These are Pima Indians," said Colonel Anza. "They are friendly." The Indians brought food.

The caravan stayed there for three days. Felipe filled water kegs and helped with the animals. One day the Indians gave a feast. Felipe ate lots of beans and corn. One man helped him cut some watermelon for Filomena, but she didn't like it. So Felipe ate her piece.

The caravan moved on through the desert. Cold winds blew sand and dust. Now there was almost no water, and no grass for the animals. Only Filomena found a few weeds to eat.

It was so cold that Felipe and Filomena slept together to keep warm. The other animals stood all night, hungry and cold, with their backs to the wind.

One morning, Felipe saw nine mules dead. Colonel Anza said sadly, "No food, no water. It is a miracle that any are alive."

Felipe walked beside his tired horse. The cold wind whipped his face. He saw starving animals fall and die.

That night, Uncle Carlos said, "We must dig holes in the dry river to get water for the animals."

Felipe told Filomena, "I must help the men tonight, but you will stay warm." He asked his cousins, "Who wants to sleep with Filomena?"

"I do!" they all cried.

Felipe saw something strange. "What is that white stuff?" he asked.

"Snow," said Colonel Anza. "You never saw snow where you lived in Mexico." That night, they sat around tiny campfires wrapped in blankets. But they were still cold.

Next morning, the sky was clear. Felipe saw distant mountains all white with snow. "California is nothing but ice and snow!" cried Uncle Carlos. "At home, we were poor but at least we were warm!"

But the sun felt warm on Felipe's shoulders. "Look," cried cousin Ruben, "the snow is melting a little!" "EEEEEAW—ee—AW!" cried Filomena. The mountains were just ahead. She smelled water bubbling from the mountain springs. She smelled winter grass growing in the valleys. The horses walked faster.

That afternoon, they came to the start of the mountains. There was water for everyone, and rich grass for the animals. "We made it!" shouted Felipe. Felipe helped unload the tired animals and led them to the grass.

"That was the hard part," cried Colonel Anza. "The rest will be easy."

They rested for a week. Then they climbed into the mountains. Tall trees and green grass grew everywhere. Felipe found sunflowers and wild grapes. The sun was bright on the river, and there were plenty of fish.

"But where is California?" Felipe asked.

"This is California!" said Colonel Anza. "We are almost at San Gabriel."

"Look at how Filomena has grown!" cried Ruben.

"Her shoulder is as tall as Felipe now!" said Aunt Maria.

"EEEEEAW—ee—AW!" sang Filomena proudly. She let Felipe climb on her back. Her muscles were strong. She trotted in a little circle, showing off.

"Our cowboy has a horse!" cried Uncle Carlos.

"She will pull logs when we build our new house!" cried Ruben.

"And plow!" cried Uncle Carlos.

"Easy there!" said Aunt Maria. "Don't work our little friend too hard!" She rubbed Filomena's nose.

At last they came through the mountains. They saw green hills rolling away to the sea. The fathers of the Mission of San Gabriel came to meet them.

"We are home at last," Felipe whispered to Filomena. And Filomena sang, "EEEEEAW—ee—AW—ee—AW!"

*The story you just read was based upon a real event. Colonel Juan Bautista de Anza was sent to open a land route from Spanish Mexico to the territory that is now California. Settlers such as those in this story left Mexico in April of 1775 and reached San Gabriel in January of 1776. Later, Colonel Anza went back to Mexico, but the families stayed in California. Their relatives live there to this day.*

## Questions

1. What did Colonel Anza say each family would get if they went to California?

2. What made Colonel Anza change his mind about Filomena?

3. What do you think was the hardest part of the journey? Explain why.

4. How would you feel if you were to move? What things would you miss most? What would you look forward to?

## Applying Reading Skills
### Plot and Setting

Use complete sentences to answer the questions below.

1. In what setting does the story take place?

2. When does the story take place?

3. If you were telling the story to a friend, what important events in the plot would you describe?

# WRITING activity

## BOOK REPORT

### Prewrite

Book reports are one way to interest people in reading a story. An ordinary book report usually names the characters and tells the main ideas in the story plot. A more interesting kind of book report retells the story from the point of view of a character in the story.

You are going to write a book report on "Felipe and Filomena." You may choose to retell the story as if you were Felipe or the little burro, Filomena. Read the story again. Think as you read how Felipe or Filomena might tell the story of their trip.

Make notes on these ideas for your book report.

1. How would my character tell about the other story characters? Filomena might say:
   "I am Filomena, a small burro who belongs to a young boy, Felipe. Felipe, his family, and I live in a poor village in Mexico in the 1700s."

2. How would my character tell about Colonel Anza's visit to the village?

3. How would my character tell about the trip?
   a. What was the most exciting part of the trip?
   b. What things happened before that part?
   c. What happened after that part?

**Write**

1. Reread the notes you made for your report.
2. Your first paragraph will tell about the characters in the story. Remember you are writing as if you were a character in the story. Use pronouns such as *I, me, mine,* and *our.*
3. Your other paragraphs will tell about Colonel Anza's visit and the trip.
4. Try to use Vocabulary Treasures in your report.
5. Now write the first draft of your report.

---

**Vocabulary Treasures**

clumsy           starving
discouraged   terrified

---

**Revise**

Read your report. Have a friend read it too. Think about this checklist as you revise.

1. A book report should interest people in reading the story. Did you tell too much? What could you take out and still tell the main ideas?
2. One way to make your report interesting is to tell some funny things. What would Filomena think was funny? What about Felipe? What funny thing could you choose to add to your report?
3. Did you choose some adjectives that would help your readers imagine the trip clearly?
4. Check your spelling and use of capital letters.
5. Now rewrite your book report to share.

# The White *Stallion*

## *Elizabeth Shub*

This story takes place in 1845. In that year, Texas became part of the United States. Many settlers made their way West to the huge new state. Texas was very different from the states they came from. There, wild horses roamed the plains.

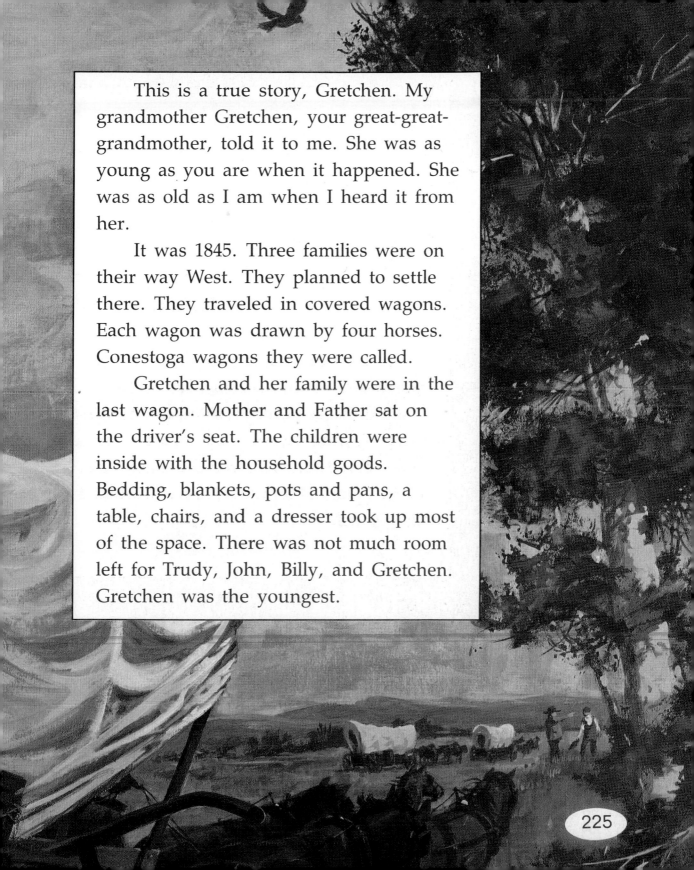

This is a true story, Gretchen. My grandmother Gretchen, your great-great-grandmother, told it to me. She was as young as you are when it happened. She was as old as I am when I heard it from her.

It was 1845. Three families were on their way West. They planned to settle there. They traveled in covered wagons. Each wagon was drawn by four horses. Conestoga wagons they were called.

Gretchen and her family were in the last wagon. Mother and Father sat on the driver's seat. The children were inside with the household goods. Bedding, blankets, pots and pans, a table, chairs, and a dresser took up most of the space. There was not much room left for Trudy, John, Billy, and Gretchen. Gretchen was the youngest.

Behind the wagon walked Anna, their old mare. She was not tied to the wagon but followed faithfully. She carried two sacks of cornmeal on her back.

It was hot in the noonday sun. The children were cranky and bored. The wagon cover shaded them, but little air came in through the openings at front and back.

John and Billy started in on each other. Trudy, the oldest, who was trying to read, asked them to be good. Their quarrel was stopped by Father's voice.

"Quick, everybody, look out! There's a herd of mustangs."

The children rushed to the back of the wagon. In the distance they could see the wild horses. The horses galloped swiftly and, in minutes, were out of sight.

"Look at Anna," John said.

The old mare stood still. She had turned her head toward the mustangs. Her usually floppy ears were lifted high. The wagon had moved some distance before Anna trotted after it.

It was hotter than ever inside.

"Father," Gretchen called, "may I ride on Anna for a while?"

Father stopped the wagon and came to the back. He lifted Gretchen onto the mare. The meal sacks made a comfortable seat. He tied her securely so that she would not fall off.

As they moved on, Gretchen fell asleep in the warmth of the sun. They were following a trail in Texas along the Guadaloupe River. The rear wheel of the first wagon hit a boulder, and the axle broke. The whole train stopped. Anna strayed away, with Gretchen sleeping on her back. No one noticed.

The travelers made camp. Children were sent for firewood and for water from the river. The women prepared food. It was not until the axle had been fixed and they were ready to eat that Gretchen and Anna were missed.

The men tried to follow the mare's tracks but soon lost them. It was getting dark. There was nothing to do but remain where they were. They would search again at the first sign of light. Faithful Anna, they thought, would return. She probably had found a rich patch of grass. She would come back when she had eaten all she wanted.

Gretchen awoke to the sound of lapping. Anna was drinking noisily from a stream. A short distance away stood a herd of ten or twelve wild horses. They were brownish in color. Some had darker brown stripes down their backs. Others had dark markings on their legs. They were mares.

After Anna had finished drinking, she moved toward them. They trotted up to her as if to say hello. Then they crossed necks with Anna. They were so friendly that Gretchen was not afraid. She did not realize that Anna had wandered far from the wagon train.

Suddenly the horses began to nibble at the sacks on Anna's back. They had smelled the cornmeal. In their eagerness they nipped Gretchen's legs. Gretchen screamed. She tried to move out of the way. She tried to loosen the ropes that tied her, but she could not free herself.

Out of nowhere a great white stallion appeared. He pranced and whinnied. He swished his long white tail. He stood on his hind legs, his white mane flying.

The mares moved quickly out of his way. The white stallion came up to Anna. He carefully bit through the ropes that tied Gretchen. Then, gently, he took hold of the back of her dress with his teeth and lifted her to the ground. He seemed to motion to the mares with his head, and then he galloped away.

229

The mares followed at once, and Anna followed them. Gretchen was left alone. She did not know what to do. "Father will find me soon," she said out loud to comfort herself. She was hungry, but there was nothing to eat. She walked to the stream and drank some water. Then she sat down on a rock to wait.

Gretchen waited and waited, but there was no sign of Father, and no sign of Anna. The sun went down. It began to get dark.

"Anna!" Gretchen called. "Anna! Anna! Anna!"

There was no answering sound. She heard a coyote howl. She heard the rustling of leaves and the call of redbirds. Gretchen began to cry. She made a place for herself on some dry leaves near a tree trunk. She curled up against the tree, and cried until she fell asleep.

Morning light woke Gretchen. The stream sparkled in the sunlight. Gretchen washed her face and drank the clear water. She looked for Anna. She called her name, but Anna did not come. Gretchen was so hungry that she tried to eat some grass, but it had a nasty taste.

She sat on her rock near the stream. She looked at the red bite marks on her legs and began to cry again. A squirrel came by. It looked at her in such a funny way that she stopped crying. She walked along the stream. She knew she must not go far. "If you are lost," Mother had warned, "stay where you are. That will make it easier to find you." Gretchen walked back to her rock.

It was afternoon when she heard the sound of hooves. A moment later Anna trotted up to the stream. The sacks of meal were gone. As the old mare took a drink of water, Gretchen hugged and patted her. Anna would find her way back to the wagon train.

Gretchen tried to climb on Anna's back, but even without the sacks the mare was too high. There was a fallen tree not far away. Gretchen wanted to use it as a step. She tugged at Anna, but Anna would not move. Gretchen pulled and pushed, but Anna stood firm.

Now again the white stallion appeared. Again he lifted Gretchen by the back of her dress and sat her on Anna's back. He nuzzled and pushed the old mare. Anna began to walk.

The white stallion walked close behind Anna for a few steps. Then, as if to say goodbye, he stood on his hind legs, whinnied, and galloped away.

Gretchen always believed the white stallion had told Anna to take her back to the wagon train. For that is what Anna did.

Your great-great-grandmother Gretchen had the scars of the wild mare bites for the rest of her life. I know because when she told me the story, she pulled down her stockings. And I saw them.

## Questions

1. What happened right after the wagon train stopped?

2. Why didn't anyone notice right away that Anna and Gretchen were gone?

3. Do you think Anna was as faithful as Gretchen's family thought her to be? Why or why not?

4. Could the events in this story really have happened? Explain your answer.

## Applying Reading Skills
### Predict Outcomes

Use complete sentences to answer the questions about "The White Stallion."

1. What do you think Gretchen's family did the morning after they discovered she was missing?

2. How did you know that Anna would probably come back to take Gretchen to the wagon train?

3. How did the storyteller know that Gretchen had really been bitten by the wild mare?

# SKILLS activity

## MAIN IDEA

A **paragraph** is a group of sentences. The sentences all tell about one thing. The main idea sentence tells the most important idea. The detail sentences tell about the main idea.

**ACTIVITY A**  Read the paragraph below. Then read the numbered questions. Choose the answer and write it on your paper.

George Washington was a man who did many things in his life. He was a surveyor who plotted the land. He was a farmer. He was a soldier and a general. Then he became the first president of the United States.

1. What is the main idea sentence?
   a. He was a farmer.
   b. George Washington was a man who did many things in his life.

2. Which detail sentence tells about what George Washington did during the war?
   a. He was a soldier and a general.
   b. He was a surveyor who plotted the land.

**ACTIVITY B**  Read the paragraph. Then write the answer to each question on your paper.

You can learn many things by reading history. You can learn what your town or state was like long ago. You can learn where the first people who settled there came from. You can find out about the clothes people wore and the homes they lived in.

1. What is the main idea sentence?
   a. You can learn many things by reading history.
   b. You can learn where the first people who settled there came from.

2. Which detail sentence talks about your town or state?
   a. You can find out about the clothes people wore and the homes they lived in.
   b. You can learn what your town or state was like long ago.

**ACTIVITY C**  Write this main idea sentence.

Early settlers often had difficult journeys to their new homes.

Now choose detail sentences that go with the main idea sentence. Write them on your paper.

1. Their planes were very small.
2. Often there wasn't enough food or water.
3. They had to face scary wild animals.
4. There was no place to buy gas.

# Wagon Wheels

## Barbara Brenner

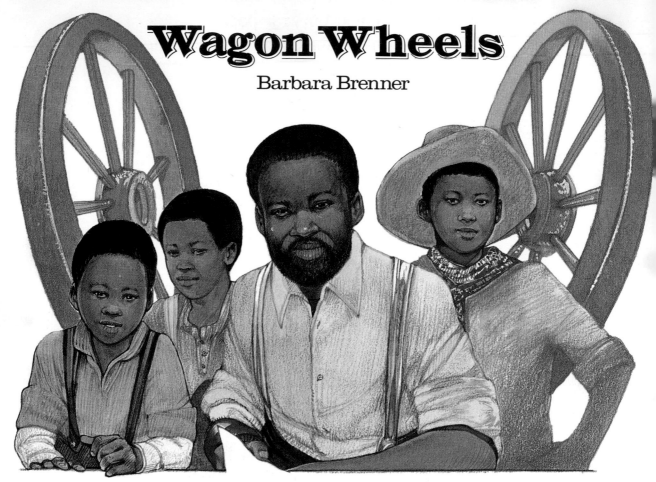

*In 1862, the United States government passed the Homestead Act. This was a law that promised free land to anyone who was willing to settle the West. Thousands of pioneers left the South when they heard about the Homestead Act. Many settled in Kansas. This is the true story of one such family, the Muldies.*

"There it is, boys," Daddy said. "Across this river is Nicodemus, Kansas, where we're going to build our house. There is free land for everyone here in the West. All we have to do is go and get it."

We had come all the way from Kentucky to get to Kansas. It had been a hard trip, and a sad one because Mama died on the way. Now there were just the four of us—Daddy, Willie, Little Brother, and me.

"Come on, boys," Daddy called. "Let's put our feet on free dirt."

We crossed the river, wagon and all. A man was waiting for us on the other side.

"I'm Sam Hickman," he said. "Welcome to the town of Nicodemus."

"Why, thank you, Brother," Daddy said. "But where *is* your town?"

"Right here," Mr. Hickman said.

We didn't see any houses, but we saw smoke coming out of holes in the prairie. "Holes in the ground are for rabbits and snakes, not for free black people," Daddy said. "I'm a carpenter and I can build fine wood houses for this town."

"No time to build wood houses now," Mr. Hickman told my Daddy. "Winter is coming, and winter in Kansas is *mean*. Better get yourself a dugout before the ground freezes."

Daddy knew Sam Hickman was right, so we got our shovels and we dug a dugout.

It wasn't much of a place—dirt floor, dirt walls, no windows, and the roof was just grass and branches. But we were glad to have that dugout when the wind began to whistle across the prairie.

Every night Willie lit the lamp and made a fire. I cooked a rabbit stew or fried a pan of fish fresh from the river.

After supper Daddy would always say, "How about a song or two?" He would take out his banjo and *Plink-a-plunk! Plink-a-plunk!* Pretty soon that dugout felt like home.

Winter came, and that Kansas winter *was* mean. It snowed day after day and we couldn't hunt or fish. We had no more rabbit stew and no more fish fresh from the river. All we had was cornmeal mush to eat.

Then one day there was no more cornmeal, and not a lick of food in the whole town of Nicodemus. There was nothing left to burn for firewood.

Little Brother cried all the time—he was so cold and hungry. Daddy wrapped blankets around him. "Hush, baby son," he said to him, "and try to sleep. Supply train will be coming soon."

But the supply train didn't come, not that day or the next.

On the third day we heard the sound of horses. Daddy looked out to see who it was.

"Indians!" he cried.

We were *so* scared because we had all heard stories about Indians. I tried to be brave. We watched from the dugout to see what they would do. Everyone in Nicodemus was watching the Indians.

First they made a circle, and then each Indian took something from his saddlebag and dropped it on the ground. The Indians turned and rode straight toward the dugouts.

"They're coming for us!" Willie cried.

We raised our guns, but the Indians rode right past us and kept on going.

We waited a long time to be sure they were gone. Then everyone ran out into the snow to see what the Indians had left.

It was FOOD!

Everyone talked at once.

"Look!"

"Fresh deer meat!"

"Fish!"

"Dried beans and squash and bundles of sticks to keep our fires burning!"

There was a feast in Nicodemus that night. But before we ate, Daddy said to us, "Johnny, Willie, Little Brother, I want you to remember this day. When someone says bad things about Indians, tell them the Osage Indians saved our lives in Nicodemus."

241

When spring came, Daddy said, "Boys, this prairie is too flat for me. I want to find land with trees and hills, so I'm going to move on. You have shelter and friends here, so I want you boys to stay. I'll send for you when I find a place."

We all listened as Daddy told us, "There's cornmeal for your bread and salt for your meat and some molasses for a sweet. You be good boys, you hear? Take care of Little Brother, and never let him out of your sight." There were tears in Daddy's eyes when he said good-bye to us.

We did what our Daddy told us. We hunted, fished, cooked, and swept the dugout clean.

We even baked our own corn bread, and we never did let Little Brother out of our sight. We made him a wagon out of an old box. Mrs. Sadler gave us wheels for it. We put Little Brother in the wagon, and pulled him along with us. You could hear the wheels squeak a mile away.

When people in Nicodemus heard that sound, they always said, "There go the Muldie boys."

April, May, and June went by. We hunted and fished and waited for a letter from Daddy, but nothing came.

Then in July the post rider came with a letter for us. It said:

Dear boys,

I have found fine free land near Solomon City. There is wood here to build a house, and good black dirt for growing corn and beans.

There is a map with this letter that shows where I am and where you are.

Follow the map, and stay close to the Solomon River until you come to the deer trail.

You will find me. I know you can do it because you are my fine big boys.

Love to you all,
Daddy

The next day we piled corn bread and blankets into Little Brother's wagon until there was no room for Little Brother.

"Can you walk like a big boy?" I asked him. He nodded.

All of Nicodemus came out to say good-bye. "Poor babies," they said. "Going a hundred fifty miles all by themselves."

But we knew we could do it because our Daddy had told us so. We went to the river, and we followed the map. We walked all day. When Little Brother got tired, I carried him.

At night we stopped and made a fire. I told Willie, "We'll take turns. First I'll watch the fire and you sleep. Fire the gun sometimes to scare wild animals away."

There were plenty of wild animals on the prairie: wolves, panthers, coyotes. Each night our fire and the sound of the guns kept them away.

But one night I heard Willie call to me, "Johnny, wake up, but don't move."

When I opened my eyes I saw a big prairie rattlesnake on the ground next to me. It was warming itself by the fire.

I didn't move. I didn't *breathe*, for fear it would bite me.

"What shall we do?" Willie whispered. I tried to think what Daddy would do, and then I remembered Daddy once told me that snakes like warm places.

I said to Willie, "Let the fire go out."

It seemed like *hours* we were there—Willie, Little Brother, and me—staying so still.

At last the fire went out. The night air got chilly and the snake moved away into the darkness.

After twenty-two days of following the river, we came to a deer trail. It led away from the river, just like on the map.

"This way," I told my brothers.

We walked along the trail that led up a hill. On the side of the hill we saw a little house with a garden in front. We could see corn growing and a man was coming out of the house. When he saw us, he began to run toward us.

"Daddy!"

"Willie! Johnny! Little Brother!"

Then there was such hugging and kissing and talking and crying and laughing and singing that . . . I bet they heard us all the way back in Nicodemus!

And Mrs. Sadler must have said, "Sounds like the Muldie boys have found their Daddy!"

## Questions

1. Why did the Muldies have to dig a dugout to live in?

2. How did the people of Nicodemus feel when the Osage Indians came and left them food?

3. Why do you think the Muldie boys' Daddy left the boys in Nicodemus when he went to find land?

4. Draw a map that shows how to get from the center of your town or city to your house. Label the streets and places you know along the way.

## Applying Reading Skills
### Summarize

Read the paragraph below. Then write a summary of the paragraph. Be sure to use your own words.

After supper Daddy would always say, "How about a song or two?" He would take out his banjo and *Plink-a-plunk! Plink-a-plunk!* Pretty soon that dugout felt like home.

# PEOPLE BUILD COMMUNITIES

## John Jarolimek and Ruth Pelz

The stories in On the Move *have all been about people who were pioneers in our country. You remember that Felipe and Filomena moved from Mexico to settle in California and the Muldie family moved from Kentucky to Kansas to find free land.*

*Another way to read about history is from a textbook. "People Build Communities" is a social studies textbook selection. It tells about the history of communities in early America. When you read, look at the headings and subheadings first. They will help you remember the important points. Try to find the main ideas and supporting details as you read.*

# 1 Indians Were the First Americans

The first people in North America were the people we now usually call American Indians. Sometimes they are called Native Americans. A native is a person who was born in a place. The words Native American remind us that these were the first people on our continent.

## The First Americans

There are many different groups of Indian people. Indian groups are often called tribes. Each tribe once spoke a different language. The Indian groups were different in other ways, too. They had different beliefs and customs. They had different ways of meeting their basic needs.

This painting shows parts of the culture of the Sioux Indians. How can you tell that horses were important to the Sioux way of life?

Indian groups had different cultures. A culture is the way of life of a group of people. All people have a culture. The food we eat and the clothing we wear are part of our culture. Our language and the things we believe are part of our culture.

## Many Different Cultures

The Indian groups met all their basic needs from the land around them. The ways they met their needs depended on their location and their culture. The tribes built houses from the materials they found in their area. They ate the plants and animals that lived in the area. The customs of Indian tribes were not the same from one part of America to another.

The map on the next page shows the location of just some of the many Indian tribes of North America. The cultures of all the tribes in the same area were very much alike. The map shows the main culture areas on our continent when only Indian people lived here. Each culture area is shown in a different color.

ARCTIC OCEAN

*Tanaina*

ESKIMO

FAR NORTH

HUDSON
BAY

*Tlingit*

*Haida*

**NORTHWEST
COAST**

*Kwakiutl*

*Makah*

*Cree*

*Chinook*

*Chippewa*

*Algonquin*

**CALIFORNIA-
INTERMOUNTAIN**

*Crow*

*Shoshoni*

*Tillamook*

**PLAINS**

*Sioux*

*Iroquois*

*Wampanoag*

*Pomo*

*Cheyenne*

*Pawnee*

*Arapaho*

*Illinois*

*Paiute*

*Delaware*

*Ute*

*Powhatan*

*Navajo*

**EASTERN
WOODLANDS**

*Mohave*

*Hopi*

*Shawnee*

*Cherokee*

**SOUTHWEST**

*Chickasaw*

*Zuni*

*Apache*

*Pueblo*

*Comanche*

*Choctaw*

*Creek*

**NORTHERN
MEXICO**

*Seminole*

PACIFIC OCEAN

ATLANTIC OCEAN

GULF OF MEXICO

*Aztec*

*Maya*

**MIDDLE
AMERICAN**

CARIBBEAN SEA

*Zapotec*

**CARIBBEAN**

**INDIAN CULTURE AREAS**

251

0          400 Miles

0          600 Kilometers

N
W—E
S

St. Augustine is the oldest city in the United States. This fort was built when the city was a Spanish colony. There also are other old Spanish buildings in St. Augustine.

# 2 Colonists Settle America

Indians were the only people in North America for thousands of years. Then people began coming here from other countries. Some of them started colonies. A colony is a community settled by people from another country. The people who live in colonies are called colonists.

## Colonists from Many Countries

The first colonies in North America were started by people from Spain. St. Augustine, Florida, built as a Spanish colony in 1565, is now the oldest city in the United States. Today St. Augustine still has parts of the old Spanish buildings.

People from other countries in Europe also started colonies here. The most important were colonists from England and France. You can see the English, French, and Spanish colonies on the map on this page. What ocean did the European colonists have to cross to come to North America?

This is a historical map. It shows the Spanish, French, and English colonies in North America. What color on the map shows Spanish colonies? Where on the map did you look for the answer?

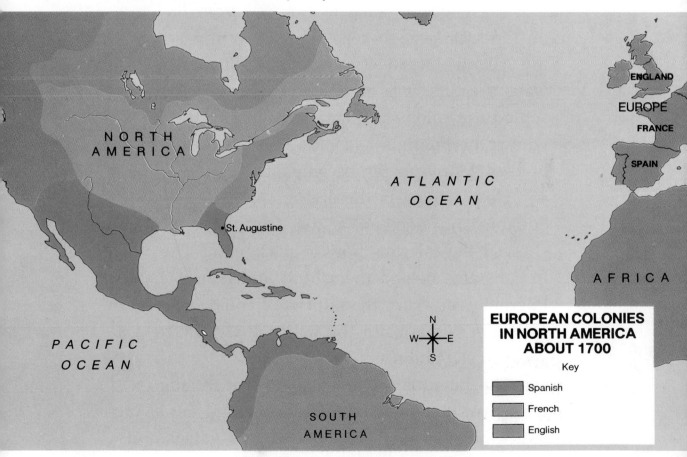

NORTH AMERICA

ATLANTIC OCEAN

•St. Augustine

PACIFIC OCEAN

SOUTH AMERICA

ENGLAND

EUROPE

FRANCE

SPAIN

AFRICA

N W E S

**EUROPEAN COLONIES IN NORTH AMERICA ABOUT 1700**

Key

Spanish

French

English

Each group of colonists brought their language and culture to the new lands. Each group also learned from the Indians who were already living on those lands. The story of the Pilgrims shows how the colonists learned from the Indians.

## The First Thanksgiving

The Pilgrims sailed to America from England on the *Mayflower* in 1620. Their long trip across the Atlantic Ocean was very hard. But in many ways their life was even more difficult when they settled the colony of Plymouth. During the first winter the Pilgrims had little food and only a few houses. Many people became sick.

Help arrived in the spring. An Indian named Squanto and members of the Wampanoag tribe showed the Pilgrims how to plant corn. The Indians also helped them hunt and fish. The Pilgrims were very thankful they could harvest, or gather, a big crop. In the fall of 1621 they held a special celebration.

The Pilgrims invited their Indian friends to join them for a feast. Everyone ate and ate at big tables full of food. Then they played games and had races. This was the first Thanksgiving.

This painting shows the artist's idea of how the Pilgrims and Indians celebrated the first Thanksgiving.

### The Colonies Become a Country

More and more people came to North America. They settled 13 colonies along the Atlantic coast. These colonies were ruled by England. But the colonists wanted to rule themselves. They wanted to be free.

On July 4, 1776, the colonists declared their independence from England. Independence is freedom from the control of others. The colonists had to fight a war against England to win their independence.

When the war was over, the colonies were free. A new country was born. Now each colony became a state. There were 13 states in the new United States of America. Americans celebrate the birth of our country every year on the Fourth of July.

# 3 The Country Grows

Many people came to the new country of the United States. New communities were formed. Cities grew up. New farms were started.

Soon there was not much good farm land left in the 13 states. But there was more farm land in the west, and it cost very little money to buy. Many families decided to move to lands in the west.

## Pioneers

People who lead the way to new lands are called pioneers. Starting a life in the new lands was hard. There were no shops or cities. There was no place to buy food or tools or clothing. There were no doctors or hospitals. Families had to make or bring along everything they needed to live.

A pioneer woman wrote this list of just some of the things her family needed for their trip west. What else would you take along?

| | | |
|---|---|---|
| flour | salt | pots and |
| sugar | medicines | dishes |
| cornmeal | seeds | rope |
| dried fruit | blankets | chickens |
| bacons and | clothing | plow |
| hams | ax and saw | horses |
| soap | rifle | |

## Traveling West

Pioneers traveled west in covered wagons. These were pulled by horses or strong cattle called oxen. Families often traveled together in a wagon train, with one covered wagon behind another in a long line.

The trip west was not easy. There were no roads across the mountains or through the forests. There were no bridges across the rivers. Sometimes pioneers built large wooden rafts to travel on a river or a lake. Rafts are flat boats. People loaded their wagons onto the rafts and floated along.

Travel was very slow. The wagon trains traveled 12 hours a day. Sometimes the pioneers had to stop to make a path for the wagons to cross. Wagons often broke or got stuck in the mud. Then other families would stop to help. The trip west might take as long as six months.

## A Busy Life

There was no time to rest when the pioneers reached the new lands. They had to cut down trees and build homes. They had to plow fields and plant their crops.

The pioneers traveled west in wagon trains. Their trip was long and hard.

Sometimes pioneer families got together with friends. Then they wore their best clothes and had a party.

Pioneer houses were small and plain. Usually they had just one or two rooms. Each house had a fireplace for cooking and heat. Pioneers did not have glass for their windows. Instead, they used pieces of cloth or deerskin.

Their main crops included wheat, corn, potatoes, fruits, and vegetables. Most families raised chickens for eggs. They got milk from their cows.

The pioneers made all their own clothing. The skins from animals they hunted were turned into leather for shoes and jackets. They made their own candles from animal fat. Soap was made from fat and ashes. Everyone in the family had jobs to do.

Pioneer life was hard, but there was still time for fun. In the evening the family sang songs or played guessing games. They also played cards and checkers. Often one family member read aloud to the others.

Homes usually were far apart, and people did not see their neighbors very often. But several times a year all the families in an area got together to have a good time.

## Pioneer Schools

The earliest pioneer communities did not have schools. Sometimes one of the mothers taught several children in her home. The other parents paid her with food they had grown or hunted.

Later, schools were built. Usually there was only one teacher in a school. Children of all ages studied in the same room. Many of them had to walk a long way to school each day. They carried their lunch in buckets. When they arrived at school they were warmed by the fire in a large stove in the classroom.

Pioneer children were too busy to go to school every day. They had to stay home to help when there was extra work to be done on the family farm. The school year usually was short.

Pioneer families lived far from their neighbors. They led a very busy life.

# Questions

1. Who were the first Americans?

2. What happened when the colonists finished fighting the war with England?

3. Why was pioneer life hard?

4. How is your life different from the life of an early pioneer?

## Applying Reading Skills
### Main Idea and Supporting Details

Find the paragraphs from "People Build Communities" listed below. Then copy each outline. Complete the outlines by writing the missing parts.

1. first paragraph under "Many Different Cultures"

MAIN IDEA:

SUPPORTING DETAILS: The tribes built houses from the materials they found in their area.

2. first paragraph under "Colonists from Many Countries"

MAIN IDEA: The first colonies in North America were started by people from Spain.

SUPPORTING DETAILS:

# Indian Children

Where we walk to school each day
Indian children used to play—
All about our native land,
Where the shops and houses stand.

And the trees were very tall,
And there were no streets at all,
Not a church and not a steeple—
Only woods and Indian people.

Only wigwams on the ground,
And at night bears prowling round—
What a different place to-day
Where we live and work and play!

*Annette Wynne*

263

# SKILLS activity

## CHARTS AND TABLES

Sometimes a writer needs to give you lots of information. Many facts and details would be hard to keep track of if they are given in a paragraph. A fast and easy way to present this kind of information is in a **chart** or **table**.

**ACTIVITY A** This table shows some cities and their populations over many years. Study the table and then answer the questions on your paper.

| Populations of some Eastern Cities | | | | | |
|---|---|---|---|---|---|
| | 1790 | 1850 | 1900 | 1950 | 1980 |
| Baltimore | 13,503 | 169,054 | 508,957 | 949,708 | 786,775 |
| Boston | 18,320 | 136,881 | 560,892 | 801,444 | 562,994 |
| Louisville | 200 | 43,194 | 204,731 | 369,129 | 298,451 |
| Norfolk | 2,959 | 14,326 | 46,624 | 213,513 | 266,979 |

1. Which city had the smallest population in 1790?
2. Which city had the smallest population in 1980?
3. Name the three cities that had a drop in their populations from 1950 to 1980.
4. Which city had the largest population in 1790?
5. How many years does this table span?

**ACTIVITY B** This chart shows some of the settlements in the United States before 1700. Look at each column and the information it tells about. Answer the questions.

| Some Settlements Before 1700 in the United States | | | |
|---|---|---|---|
| **Settlement** | **National Origin of Colonists** | **Present Day State** | **Year** |
| Breuckelen (Brooklyn) | Dutch | New York | 1646 |
| El Paso | Spanish | Texas | 1659 |
| Jamestown | English | Virginia | 1607 |
| New Amsterdam | Dutch | New York | 1623 |
| New Haven | English | Connecticut | 1636 |
| New Plymouth | English | Massachusetts | 1620 |
| Pensacola | Spanish | Florida | 1696 |
| Salem | English | Massachusetts | 1628 |
| Santa Fe | Spanish | New Mexico | 1609 |
| St. Augustine | Spanish | Florida | 1565 |

1. In what states did the Spanish found their settlements?
2. Which states had English settlements?
3. Which settlement changed its name?
4. What was the earliest settlement in the United States?

# THE TOWN THAT MOVED

## Mary Jane Finsand

*Many towns grew up in the United States during the 1700s and 1800s. Towns grew in different places for different reasons. Read to find out how a small town in northern Minnesota grew and became famous.*

Once upon a time, when the United States was still a young nation, much of the country was wilderness.

And so it was in northern Minnesota.

What was there? Forests and lakes. Bears and deer and wolves.

Some men thought there might even be gold and silver. They were not sure, but they were curious. So they went to the wilderness to seek their fortunes.

Some of these men came to hunt the animals. Then they sold the furs to people in cities far away. Others came to cut down trees and sell the lumber.

Still other men came to look for silver or gold. They did not find much of either in northern Minnesota. They did not have an easy life either!

There were no towns. There were no roads. The winters were long and cold. It was no place to bring a family. The men had to come by themselves.

Then, in August of 1891, a cyclone blew over the wilderness. The winds were fast and strong. They blew down many great trees.

Underneath, on the roots of the trees and in the holes they left behind, men discovered iron ore! There may not have been gold in northern Minnesota, but in the 1800s iron ore was almost as exciting.

Iron ore is the rock from which we get iron. In the 1800s iron was badly needed to build railroad trains and tracks.

It wasn't long before news of the iron ore in Minnesota had spread all around the country. Men began to pour into Minnesota. They came to start iron ore mines.

One of those men was named Frank Hibbing. Frank Hibbing knew that if he started an iron ore mine he would need many men to work in it. The men would want to bring their families. So Hibbing decided to build a town.

First he bought land. Then he hired men to build roads. He hired other men to build log cabins for the families.

Soon people were coming from all over the country to work in Hibbing's mine and live in his town. People even came from countries far away like Ireland, Sweden, and Germany. Many came to work in the mine, but others came to open stores. Soon there were schools and churches and banks, too.

On August 15, 1893, the people voted to become the town of Hibbing, Minnesota. Hibbing became famous for its rich iron ore. The town grew and grew. Everyone who lived there was very proud of Hibbing. They wanted to make it a beautiful city.

They built fancy theaters and lovely parks and fine houses. They started excellent schools for their children, and they took wonderful care of their town.

Then one day the mine owners made a discovery: THE VERY BEST IRON ORE WAS RIGHT BENEATH THE TOWN OF HIBBING!

Corner of Hibbing, 1920

The people of Hibbing would have to move. If they didn't, the mines would have to shut down. The miners would be out of work. Soon the other businesses would have to close down, too.

The people of Hibbing were very upset. They had worked so hard to build their beautiful town. How could they leave it? How could they watch it be torn down to make way for new mines?

"Where will we go?" they asked.

"We will build you a new town," said the mine owners.

"But what about our fine homes and our fancy theaters and our beautiful hotels?" the people asked.

The mine owners thought and thought, and finally they came up with a solution. "We will move your homes!" they said. "We will move the whole town!"

It sounded like a wonderful idea. But how on earth would they do it?

The mine owners and the people sat down together to think and talk.

"We have horses and tractors," said one man. "Maybe we could pull the buildings."

"But we can't pull big buildings along the ground," said the mayor. "They will break into pieces. We need wheels or something."

"Wheels are a problem," said the mine owners. "Most of our wheels are just not large or strong enough to move a building."

"Well," said someone else, "we certainly have lots of trees. We could cut them down, then make them smooth, and roll our houses on them."

"That's it!" everyone cried.

So the mine owners and the people began to get ready for moving day. They separated all the buildings from their basements. Then they dug new basements for all those buildings. They chopped down trees. Then they cut away the branches. They made the logs smooth.

People all over the world heard about Hibbing's plan to move.

"Impossible!" they said.

One big city newspaper wrote: "HIBBING GONE CRAZY!"

No one believed that the people of Hibbing could move their whole town.

Finally moving day arrived. The Hibbing Hotel would be the first building moved. The miners attached large chains and ropes to cranes from the mine. The cranes would be powered by steam engines. Then the chains were wrapped over and under the Hibbing Hotel. Slowly the cranes lifted the hotel. Then they swung it over and lowered it gently onto a log roller.

Next ropes and straps were wrapped around the hotel, then attached to horses up front. "Giddap! Giddap!" shouted the drivers. The horses started forward. Slowly the Hibbing Hotel rolled down the street.

As soon as the back log rolled out from under the building, people grabbed it. They strapped it to a horse and pulled it up to the front. Then they slid it underneath again.

Down the street the buildings rolled to their new locations. Day in and day out the people of Hibbing worked to save their beautiful town.

At last all the business buildings had been moved. Next would come the houses.

"What should we do with our furniture?" the women asked.

"And our toys and clothes," said the children.

"Leave everything in the houses," they were told. "And you can ride in your houses, too."

Moving a business building, around 1919

Moving a house in 1919

The very next day the first house was lifted onto logs. Down the street it came. A log was placed up front. Then a log rolled out back. That log was placed up front, and another log rolled out back.

And so it went until, one after another, 186 houses had been moved. The people of Hibbing had done it! They had moved their whole town!

Hibbing's move began in the year 1912, but the major push didn't come until 1921, and most of the buildings were moved in the 1920s. It wasn't until the fall of 1953 or the spring of 1954, though, that the very last building was finally moved.

The people of Hibbing moved their town because they loved it. It wasn't until many years later that they found they had made history. Today if you go to Hibbing you can see many of the buildings that were rolled on logs to where they now stand. And people are still proud to say, "We are from Hibbing, the town that moved!"

**Moving a house across a bridge, late 1920s**

## Questions

1. Why was the discovery of iron ore important in the 1800s?

2. Why didn't anyone believe that the people of Hibbing could move their whole town?

3. Do you think it would have been easier to build a new town rather than moving the old town? Give reasons for your answer.

4. If you were building a new town, what would you include in it?

## Applying Reading Skills
### Summarize

Read the paragraphs below. Then write a summary of each paragraph. Be sure to use your own words.

1.     Iron ore is the rock from which we get iron. In the 1800s iron was badly needed to build railroad trains and tracks.

2.     Down the street the buildings rolled to their new locations. Day in and day out the people of Hibbing worked to save their beautiful town.

# ANYTOWN, U.S.A.

Towns and cities in this country have been named for all sorts of things. When settlers first came here they named towns for the places they had left. New York was named after York, England. How do you think Germantown was named?

Mississippi and Massachusetts are Indian names. Other towns like Prairie City, Riverside, Ocean City, and Mountain View were named for how they looked. Some towns were named for products that grew there. How do you think Orange, California and Orange, Florida got their names?

Hibbing, Minnesota, was named after Frank Hibbing, the man who built the town. Other towns got their names the same way. Think about Jamestown, Johnsville, and Phillipsburg. *Ville* and *burg* mean the same as town.

Imagine that you are renaming your home town. Use the ideas below. Then, write the new names.

1. Think of a famous person from your town.
2. Think of what grows or is made in your town.
3. Think of how the area around your town looks.

# THE STORY OF
# PAUL BUNYAN

### Barbara Emberley

*This is the story of a man who was so big and so strong he could move a whole town all by himself. Perhaps this story stretches the facts a bit, but that's why this kind of story is called a tall tale. Some of the tall tales we know came from the stories loggers told as they traveled from camp to camp across the country. The story of one logger—Paul Bunyan—might just be the tallest of them all.*

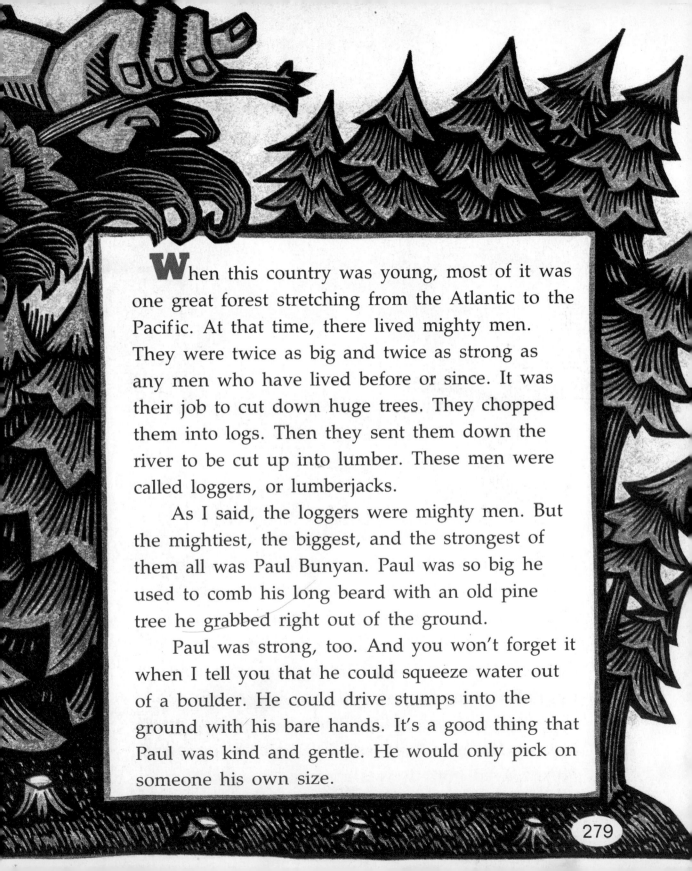

When this country was young, most of it was one great forest stretching from the Atlantic to the Pacific. At that time, there lived mighty men. They were twice as big and twice as strong as any men who have lived before or since. It was their job to cut down huge trees. They chopped them into logs. Then they sent them down the river to be cut up into lumber. These men were called loggers, or lumberjacks.

As I said, the loggers were mighty men. But the mightiest, the biggest, and the strongest of them all was Paul Bunyan. Paul was so big he used to comb his long beard with an old pine tree he grabbed right out of the ground.

Paul was strong, too. And you won't forget it when I tell you that he could squeeze water out of a boulder. He could drive stumps into the ground with his bare hands. It's a good thing that Paul was kind and gentle. He would only pick on someone his own size.

Paul used most of his strength for logging.
One time he dug himself a river to help move his
logs. Paul was cutting trees up in Minnesota. He
had to get them to the sawmill which was in
New Orleans. He decided the best way to do it
would be by river. But there was no river. So
Paul had a light lunch of: 19 pounds of sausage,
6 hams, 8 loaves of bread, and 231 flapjacks. It
was a small lunch for Paul but he counted on
eating a big supper to make up for it. Paul
dug his river that afternoon. He called it the
Mississippi. As far as I know, that is what it is
called to this day.

Once it looked like Paul was going to be too
*strong* for his own good. But it was being *smart*
that saved him. It was a good thing, too!

Paul was clearing the state of Iowa for the farmers. He wanted to get done in time for them to plant their first crop of corn. But every time he would try to make his ax cut more than six or seven trees, the handle would break. So he wove a handle of grass that worked very well. He cleared Iowa so quickly that he had time to clear Kansas, too. I think the farmers planted wheat in Kansas.

You'd think a man as big as Paul would be slow on his feet. Well, he wasn't. Why he could even beat his shadow in a race.

Of course, Paul wasn't always so big. I've been told that twelve storks brought baby Paul to his mother in Kennebunkport, Maine. He didn't weigh more than 104 or 105 pounds. Forty-six pounds of that was his black, curly beard.

**P**aul was a happy baby, but restless. Before he was more than a few weeks old he had flattened all the trees in town. He flattened a few barns with his playful kicking, too. So the folks around Kennebunkport built him a huge log cradle. Then they anchored him a few miles off shore.

This delighted Paul. But his bouncing around caused such high waves that one of the biggest towns in Maine at that time, Boston, was washed out to sea. It floated down to Massachusetts. It still is there to this day.

When Paul was older he got hold of all the books that had ever been written. He took them up to a cave in Canada and read them. Just as he finished the last book, a snowflake blew into his cave. It was the most brilliant *blue* he had ever seen.

It snowed, and snowed, and snowed. Everything was a blanket of blue. When it stopped snowing, Paul decided to take a walk.

He was down by Niagara Falls. There he noticed a big blue ox tail. It was sticking out of the snow. And what did he find on the other end of the big blue ox tail? Why he found a big blue ox! The snow had turned that ox *blue* from head to toe.

Some folks say that when the blue snow melted it turned into real blue lakes. We call them the Great Lakes. But then you can't believe *everything* you hear.

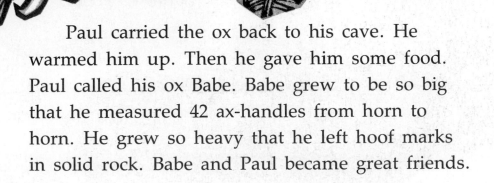

Paul carried the ox back to his cave. He warmed him up. Then he gave him some food. Paul called his ox Babe. Babe grew to be so big that he measured 42 ax-handles from horn to horn. He grew so heavy that he left hoof marks in solid rock. Babe and Paul became great friends.

With a great Blue Ox to help him, it was natural that Paul should decide to go logging. He had some of the biggest men in the woods working for him. Even the chore boy was twelve feet tall and everyone picked on him because he was too little to fight back.

Paul's crew slept in a bunkhouse. It was so tall it had a hinged chimney to let the sun go by. There was a long chow hall. It was so long that the waiters had to ride on horseback to get around. The flapjack griddle was so big, it took three sharp-eyed men four days to look across it. It took six men three days skating around it, with bacon strapped to their shoes, to get it greased.

Paul put all these buildings on runners. Then he hitched them up to Babe. They went back and forth across this great country, clearing the land. They cleared the West so the cattle could graze. They cleared Kansas for wheat and Iowa for corn. These are just a few states they worked in.

When Paul and Babe had finished their work, they went deep into the woods. There they took a good, long rest. And as far as any one knows, they are resting still.

## Questions

1. What was the job of the loggers, or lumberjacks?

2. Why did Paul and Babe become great friends?

3. What part of this tall tale do you think stretched the facts the most?

4. You have read about some of the things Paul Bunyan is said to have done. Write about something else Paul might have done and describe how he would have done it.

## Applying Reading Skills
### Summarize

Read the paragraphs below. Then write a summary of each paragraph. Be sure to use your own words.

1. You'd think a man as big as Paul would be slow on his feet. Well, he wasn't. Why he could even beat his shadow in a race.

2. He was down by Niagara Falls. There he noticed a big blue ox tail. And what did he find on the other end of the big blue ox tail? Why he found a big blue ox! The snow had turned that ox *blue* from head to toe.

# FUNNY TALK

Words can be used for communicating, for giving information, or for warning. Words can also be used to make you laugh. A **pun** is a funny or clever use of a word that has more than one meaning.

What animal keeps the best time? A watchdog!

A pun can also be the use of a word that sounds like another word but has a different meaning. Why did the house call the doctor? It had a window pane!

Read the following puns. Write them on your paper. Then match them with the correct answer.

1. What do you call a sleeping bull?
2. What do ducks do when they fly upside down?
3. When is a baseball player like a thief?
4. What did the elephant do when he hurt his toe?
5. Why is the library the tallest building?
6. Where's the best place to keep noisy dogs off the street?

a barking lot          They quack up.
He called a toe truck.  It has hundreds of stories.
a bulldozer            when he or she steals a base

# Can You TOP THIS?

Margaret H. Lippert

Tall tales such as the one about Paul Bunyan are part of American folklore. Our folklore is made up of all of the things that have been passed down from person to person over the years—even jokes and riddles. So if you've heard any of the jokes in this radio play, it's because someone has already passed them on to you!

## Characters:

Bill Baxter, teenage host of "Can You Top This?"

panelists     Mrs. Maureen Murphy

Miss Sarah Skidmore

Mr. Albert Abernathy

Mr. Peter Price

## Members of the studio audience:

| | |
|---|---|
| Jenny | Beth |
| Mike | Tony |
| Rosa | Laura |
| Charles | Hiroki |
| Other boys and girls | |

## Setting:

The radio studio of WJOK, Cincinnati, Ohio

*(A long table is located center stage. Bill Baxter is seated behind the table, with a microphone in front of him. The two ladies are seated on one side of Bill; the two gentlemen are seated on his other side. Members of the studio audience are seated facing the table.)*

**Bill:** Hello, everyone! Welcome to "Can You Top This?", the joke show produced by kids, for kids. Welcome to our studio audience, and welcome to you out there in our listening audience. This week we have with us on our panel some of the finest jokers . . . joke experts in the country. Yes, they're right here in Cincinnati for the 51st Annual All-American Joke Festival, which opens tomorrow. *(turning to the panel)* Now I understand that you are the finalists for the title of National Champion Joker.

**Mrs. Murphy, Miss Skidmore, Mr. Abernathy, Mr. Price:** Yes, that's right.

**Bill:** Well, before we get down to business today, would you introduce yourselves to our audiences? We'll start with you, Mrs. Murphy.

**Mrs. Murphy:** My name is Maureen Murphy, and I come from Jackson, Mississippi.

**Miss Skidmore:** I'm Sarah Skidmore from Sacramento, California.

**Mr. Abernathy:** Albert Abernathy here, from Ogunquit, Maine.

**Mr. Price:** Peter Price. Pittsburgh, Pennsylvania.

**Bill:** We're honored to have you with us. Now, you know the rules. You all have one crackup, uh, I mean crack at, the grand prize here on "Can You Top This?" And of course members of our studio audience are also free to compete. The listening audience, you folks there at home, will vote for the funniest joke by postcard. The winner will be announced on next week's show. All right, Mrs. Murphy, you're first.

**Mrs. Murphy:** Knock, knock.

**Studio audience:** Who's there?

**Mrs. Murphy:** Amos.

**Studio audience:** Amos who?

**Mrs. Murphy:** A mosquito bit me. *(Everyone laughs.)*

**Mrs. Murphy:** *(interrupting the laughter)* Knock, knock.

**Studio audience:** Who's there?

**Mrs. Murphy:** Andy.

**Studio audience:** Andy who?

**Mrs. Murphy:** And he bit me again. *(Everyone groans.)*

291

**Bill:** *(laughing)* That's good. That reminds me, there's something I wanted to ask you. Will you remember me in 50 years?

**Mrs. Murphy:** Yes.

**Bill:** Will you remember me in 20 years?

**Mrs. Murphy:** Yes.

**Bill:** Will you remember me in 10 years?

**Mrs. Murphy:** Yes.

**Bill:** Will you remember me in 5 years?

**Mrs. Murphy:** Yes.

**Bill:** Will you remember me next year?

**Mrs. Murphy:** Yes.

**Bill:** Will you remember me next month?

**Mrs. Murphy:** Yes.

**Bill:** Will you remember me next week?

**Mrs. Murphy:** Yes.

**Bill:** Will you remember me tomorrow?

**Mrs. Murphy:** Yes.

**Bill:** Will you remember me in another minute?

**Mrs. Murphy:** Of course.

**Bill:** Knock, knock.

**Mrs. Murphy:** Who's there?

**Bill:** You forgot me already?

**Mrs. Murphy:** *(chuckling)* You got me that time, Bill. I may forget you, but I'll never forget that joke!

**Bill:** Miss Skidmore, you're next.

**Miss Skidmore:** Here's a riddle my mother used to ask:

> There is a thing that nothing is,
> And yet it has a name;
> 'Tis sometimes tall and sometimes short,
> It joins our walk, it joins our sport,
> And plays at every game.

**Bill:** O.K. Does anyone have any ideas? *(pauses)* No?

**Miss Skidmore:** Your shadow.

**Bill:** That's a good one. I should have guessed it myself. Now I have a riddle for you:

> You use it between your head and your toes,
> The more it works, the thinner it grows.

**Miss Skidmore:** That's one my mother told me, too. The answer's a bar of soap. I didn't know any of you youngsters knew the old riddles.

293

**Bill:** We know some, but we're always ready for more. What do you have for us today, Mr. Abernathy?

**Mr. Abernathy:** I'd like to tell you folks a story. Now it's pretty scary, so hang onto your seats.

Albert was walking down Third Street out toward the country. As he was walking along and thinking, he suddenly realized that it was going to rain. He looked around for a place to take shelter. But all he could see was an old, dilapidated house that obviously was empty. Inside, everything was a shambles. But with a flash of lightning and a crash of thunder, the storm was upon him, and he knew it was too late to leave. Albert then heard a rapping sound. It seemed to come from a nearby closet. But nothing was there. As the rapping grew louder and louder, it gave Albert a very empty feeling, and his efforts to find what was making the sound became more and more frantic. After searching and searching, he finally decided that the sound was coming from a small trunk.

Although he had no trouble unfastening
the trunk, getting up enough nerve
to open it was a different matter.
However, he soon overcame his fear, jerked
open the lid, and looked inside. At last he
knew what was making the dreadful rapping
sound. It was wrapping paper.

*(Everyone laughs.)*

**Bill:** *(laughing)* Whew! You really had me scared.
Can you top that, Mr. Price?

**Mr. Price:** Well here's a story that doesn't just
end with a surprise. It has surprises all the way
through it.

'Twas midnight on the ocean.
  Not a streetcar was in sight.
And everything that you could see
  Was hidden out of sight.
'Twas a summer day in winter,
  And the snowflakes fell like glass.
A barefoot boy with shoes on
  Stood sitting in the grass.

**Bill:** Hey that's pretty tricky.

**Mr. Price:** It's what we called "tangletalk," and we used to make it up to try on our friends. I'll bet your audience could think of some funny ones, too.

**Bill:** Go to it, folks, and when you get a good one come and try it on us. Well, that wraps up *(audience laughs)* . . . the first part of our program. Now we'll take entries from our studio audience.

**Jenny:** Did you have your TV set on last week?

**Bill:** Yes.

**Jenny:** How did it fit?

*(Laughter.)*

**Mike:** *(to Jenny)* Is your refrigerator running?

**Jenny:** Yes.

**Mike:** Better go catch it!

*(Everyone groans.)*

**Rosa:** What has 4 wheels and flies? *(pauses)* A garbage truck!

*(Everyone laughs.)*

**Charles:** *(to Rosa)* What has 18 legs and catches flies?

**Rosa:** An 18-legged dragonfly?

**Charles:** No. A baseball team.

*(Laughter.)*

**Bill:** That reminds me of another baseball joke. *(to Charles)* If you were shut up in an iron house with no windows, no doors, and no other openings, and you had nothing with you but a baseball bat, how would you get out?

**Charles:** I don't know.

**Bill:** Don't you know how to play baseball? Anybody could get out if he knew how to play baseball.

**Charles:** You've got me.

**Bill:** It's simple. Three strikes and you're out.

*(Everyone giggles.)*

**Beth:** I know another one about a game. One night a man paid his friend a visit and, much to his surprise, found him playing chess with his dog. "This dog must be very intelligent to be able to play chess," he said. "Oh, he's not so smart," his friend replied. "I just beat him three games out of four."

*(Everyone laughs.)*

**Tony:** How about this one: Two horses were standing in the middle of a field discussing current events. A dog wandered over and asked, "What's new, fellows?" One of the horses turned to the other with a surprised look on his face. "Imagine that," he said, "a talking dog."

*(Everyone groans.)*

**Laura:** What has two feet and no legs? *(pauses)* Twenty-four inches.

*(Everyone laughs.)*

**Hiroki:** *(to Laura)* Who is bigger, Mr. Bigger, or Mr. Bigger's baby?

**Laura:** Mr. Bigger.

**Hiroki:** No. The baby is a little Bigger.

*(Everyone laughs.)*

**Bill:** Well, folks, I wish we had a little bigger time slot for this program *(everyone groans)*, but that will have to be it until next week when we'll be back with more sidesplitting jokes for you. So long now. Don't forget to send your votes to me, at WJOK, Box 1234, Cincinnati, Ohio. The grand prize is the best book of jokes in the world, *Tickling Your Funnybone*, by your host, BILL BAXTER!

**Studio audience:** Yea!

**Bill:** I know you can't top THAT!

## Questions

1. What is the setting of the play?

2. Which panel member was the riddle expert?

3. Explain why Mr. Price's story is called "tangletalk."

4. If you were a member of the audience, what joke would you share?

## Applying Reading Skills
### Predict Outcomes

Use complete sentences to answer these questions about "Can You Top This?".

1. How would you have known the answer to Miss Skidmore's riddle before she gave the answer?

2. Who do you think will receive the title of National Champion Joker?

3. Write a joke from the story to which you guessed the answer. How did you guess the answer?

## SKILLS activity

### PREDICT OUTCOMES

Sometimes you can tell before a story is over how it will end. When you think you know how a story will end, you are "predicting the outcome" of the story.

**ACTIVITY A** Read the part of a story below. The story is not finished. Something else will happen.

Paul Bunyan was so big he could not fit inside most people's houses. He would have to visit people outside. One day he went to visit some friends outside their house. Then it started to rain. Paul Bunyan pulled the roof off the house.

How do you think the story will end? Choose one of the answers below and write it on your paper.

a. Paul Bunyan held the roof over everyone like a huge umbrella.
b. Paul Bunyan ran away with the roof.

**ACTIVITY B**  Now read the story parts on this page. Think how each one might end. Choose an answer and write it on your paper.

When he heard that gold had been discovered in California, Jim Smith left his home. He rode his horse across two states. He arrived in California in the morning. He stopped the first person he saw.

a.  Jim asked the man where gold had been found.
b.  Jim traded horses with the man.

The Macks love the house they have lived in for years. They have bought some land in another town. A hole has been dug on the land. The movers come and lift up their house.

a.  Then they paint the house red.
b.  Then they move the house across town.

Babe the Blue Ox was the biggest animal anyone had ever seen. One day he was very hungry. He went looking for food. He came to a huge field of grass.

a.  He walked past the field.
b.  He ate every blade of grass in the field.

# THE OX-CART MAN

Donald Hall                    Illustrated by Barbara Cooney

*This story came about in the folklore tradition. The author heard the story from his cousin. His cousin said he had heard it when he was a boy from an old man. The old man told him that he had heard it when he was a boy, from an old man. Now the story is being passed on to you.*

In October he backed his ox into his cart and he and his family filled it up with everything they made or grew all year long that was left over.

He packed a bag of wool he sheared from the sheep in April.

He packed a shawl his wife wove on a loom from yarn spun at the spinning wheel from sheep sheared in April.

He packed five pairs of mittens his daughter knit from yarn spun at the spinning wheel from sheep sheared in April.

He packed candles the family made.

He packed linen made from the flax they grew.

He packed shingles he split himself.

He packed birch brooms his son carved with a borrowed kitchen knife.

He packed potatoes they dug from their garden—but first he counted out potatoes enough to eat all winter and potatoes for seed next spring.

He packed a barrel of apples, honey and honeycombs, turnips and cabbages.

He packed a wooden box of maple sugar from the maples they tapped in March when they boiled and boiled and boiled the sap away.

He packed a bag of goose feathers that his children collected from the barnyard geese.

When his cart was full, he waved good-bye to his wife, his daughter, and his son.

He walked at his ox's head ten days over hills, through valleys, by streams, past farms and villages, until he came to Portsmouth and Portsmouth Market.

He sold the bag of wool.

He sold the shawl his wife made.

He sold five pairs of mittens.

He sold candles and shingles.

He sold birch brooms.

He sold potatoes.

He sold apples.

He sold honey and honeycombs, turnips and cabbages.

He sold maple sugar.

He sold a bag of goose feathers.

Then he sold the wooden box he carried the apples in.

Then he sold the bag he carried the potatoes in.

Then he sold his ox cart.

Then he sold his ox, and kissed him good-bye on his nose.

Then he sold his ox's yoke and harness.

With his pockets full of coins, he walked through Portsmouth Market.

He bought an iron kettle to hang over the fire at home.

For his daughter he bought an embroidery needle that came all the way from England.

For his son he bought a Barlow knife, for
carving birch brooms with.

For the whole family he bought two pounds
of wintergreen peppermints.

Then he walked home, with the needle and
the knife and the wintergreen peppermints tucked
into the kettle, and a stick over his shoulder,
stuck through the kettle's handle, and coins still
in his pockets.

He walked past farms and villages,
over hills, through valleys, by streams, until he
came to his farm, and his son, his daughter, and
his wife were waiting for him.

His daughter took her needle and began stitching.

His son took his Barlow knife and started whittling.

They cooked dinner in their new kettle, and afterward everyone ate a wintergreen peppermint.

That night the ox-cart man sat in front of his fire stitching a new harness for the young ox in the barn.

He carved a new yoke and sawed planks for
a new cart and split shingles all winter.

His wife made flax into linen all winter.

His daughter embroidered linen all winter.

His son carved Indian brooms from birch all
winter, and everybody made candles.

In March they tapped the sugar maple trees
and boiled the sap down.

In April they sheared the sheep, spun yarn, and wove and knitted.

In May they planted potatoes, turnips, and cabbages, while apple blossoms bloomed and fell, while bees woke up, starting to make new honey, and geese squawked in the barnyard, dropping feathers as soft as clouds.

## Questions

1. What were three of the things the ox-cart man packed in his cart?

2. Why didn't the ox-cart man keep his ox and cart?

3. What do you think the ox-cart man and his family did from June to September?

4. Describe something you do with your family at the same time each year.

## Applying Reading Skills
### Plot and Setting

Use complete sentences to answer the questions below.

1. Where did the man go to sell his things?

2. How long does it take the man to get to market?

3. If you were telling the story to a friend, what important events in the plot would you describe?

# THE CABIN
# FACED WEST

JEAN FRITZ

In the early 1780s, Ann Hamilton moved with her family to the wilderness of Western Pennsylvania, or Western Country as the pioneers called it. Ann noticed that even their cabin on Hamilton Hill faced west.

The new life was hard for Ann. She missed her cousin Margaret, her school, and her friends back on the other side of the Allegheny Mountains in Gettysburg. In the Western Country, good times and special events had to wait for "some day."

To keep herself company, Ann kept a diary. It had a deerskin cover, like a real frontier diary, but inside it was filled with thoughts of her old life in Gettysburg. This part of Ann's story begins on a day where everything has gone wrong for Ann. But a surprise visitor changes Ann's day and even her thinking about her new life as a pioneer.

It certainly wasn't her day, Ann thought crossly as she took an empty pail and went out the cabin door. But when she reached the road that led from Gettysburg, she wondered. Maybe, after all, something might yet turn the day her way. The road seemed to have more magic to it than she had ever known. The sun's rays slanted down on it as though they were lighting up a stage where something important was going to happen. There was a difference in the mood of the road. It wasn't a happy, dancing mood, nor a mysterious, moonlight mood. Today there was a grandness to the road, as though it were a carpet unfurling over the hill before some glorious secret. As Ann stood in the middle of the road, holding her pail in front of her, two golden leaves drifted down, turning slowly over and over in the air, and settled in the bottom of her pail. A wild goose dipped low, honking, from the sky, like a herald sent ahead with news.

Ann walked down the hill, captured by the spell of the road. As she rounded each bend, she found herself half expecting something wonderful to be waiting on the other side. She didn't know what, but something. From time to time she stopped to pick grapes that had survived the storm.

On all the hill, the only sounds were the plopping
of grapes in her pail and the occasional long
honk of a passing goose. Ann followed the road
as it wound its way down the hill, turning corner
after corner, looking for grapes but secretly hoping
for something she couldn't even put into words.

Her pail was almost full when she suddenly noticed where she was. She was almost to the bottom of the hill. Almost to the spot her brother David had pointed out as the site for the first church. She had let the road lead her farther than she had ever gone alone. Instead of something wonderful lying around the next corner of the road, there was probably something dreadful.

And then Ann heard hoofbeats. They were coming from the east—not just one horse but three or four, and they were not far away.

Ann ducked down behind some tall grass by the side of the road and made herself into the smallest ball she could possibly squeeze into, wrapping her arms tightly around her knees. She held her breath as the first horse rounded the bend of the road. She must not move—not even a finger. She kept her eyes on the road, counting the legs of the horses as they came into sight. Now there were two horses . . . three . . . four. If four men were traveling together from the East to the West at this time of year, they were probably not settlers. They were likely up to no good. They must be the Doane gang that David had warned her about.

All at once Ann began to tremble all over. The first horse had stopped on the road in front of her. Then the other horses came to a stop. As Ann peeped out between the tall grasses, all she could see was a forest of horse legs. From some place way up high above the legs of the first horse came a deep voice. "Little girl," it said, "I wonder if you could tell me what your mother is having for dinner tonight."

The voice didn't sound like the voice of a horse thief. Slowly Ann lifted her eyes from the legs of the horse to the boots of the rider. Slowly she lifted them to the place where the voice had come from. Then she found herself looking into the most wonderful face she had ever seen.

It was a strong face, kind and good, and there was something strangely familiar about it. It was as if Ann ought to know this man, as if she almost knew him. No matter what David had said about strangers, somehow Ann knew deep inside that he hadn't been talking about this one. She stopped feeling afraid. She stood up.

"My mother is having peas and potatoes and corn bread for our evening meal," she said, "and she's baking pumpkin pie."

The man smiled. He leaned down toward Ann. "Would you tell her," he said, "that General George Washington would like to take supper with her?"

For a moment Ann could not believe her ears. General Washington on Hamilton Hill! Then all at once she knew it was true. This was the way she had pictured George Washington from what her friend, Arthur Scott, had said about him. This must have been just how Washington looked, riding among the men at Valley Forge. Suddenly Arthur Scott's words flashed into her mind. "He always seemed to be there just when our courage began to peter out."

Ann swallowed hard. She tried to drop a curtsy but it turned out to be just a stiff little bob. She tried to find her voice, but it didn't turn out any better than the curtsy. It was more like a squeak. "My mother will be pleased," she said. "I'll tell her."

Then Ann found herself and her pail of grapes up on the saddle in front of one of the men in General Washington's party. He said he was Dr. Craik, a friend of the General's, but Ann didn't pay much attention. She didn't even look at the other men. All she could see was the white horse in front of her and the straight back of General Washington going up Hamilton Hill. The road itself seemed almost to be moving them up the hill in a kind of magic dream. Except it wasn't a dream, Ann reminded herself. It was true—gloriously, wonderfully true. For some unbelievable reason, General George Washington was on the western side of the mountains and he was going to have supper on Hamilton Hill.

Suddenly Ann turned to Dr. Craik. "Why did General Washington come here?" she asked.

"He owns land in this county," Dr. Craik replied. "He's come to check on it."

"He owns land *here*—in Washington County?" Ann repeated.

Dr. Craik smiled. "Yes, he can't move here, but he bought land because he believes in this part of the country. Some day this land will be worth a great deal of money. He wants to do all he can to develop this side of the mountains."

Ann fell silent, her eyes on General Washington. Again she pictured him at Valley Forge. A lot of people hadn't believed in a free and independent country, she thought. But Washington had. And now he believed in the Western Country. It wasn't just fathers and brothers and settlers who believed in it and owned land here. *George Washington did too.*

Ann and Dr. Craik jogged up the hill. The other men called back and forth to each other, but Ann didn't hear them.

Afterward Ann could never remember just how she introduced General Washington and his friends to her mother. When she caught her breath again, they had started on a tour of the farm with David. Ann and her mother were alone in the cabin with supper to prepare.

Mrs. Hamilton's eyes were shining as she stepped away from the door. "Now is the time to use the linen tablecloth, Ann," she said, "and the lavender flowered plates."

Ann was standing in the doorway, her head in the clouds, watching the men put up their horses. At her mother's words, she came quickly down to the world. What a wonderful world it was, she thought, as she flew over to her mother's chest for the linen tablecloth.

"The food is almost ready," Mrs. Hamilton said. "I'll take care of that while you set the table."

Ann spread out the white linen cloth on the table. She smoothed it gently over the rough boards. She pulled it to hang even on all sides. She unwrapped nine flowered plates and placed them around the table. She put knives, forks, and spoons at each place and set new tall candles in the center of the table.

Then Ann stepped back to look at what she had done. Somehow the whole room seemed changed; it seemed larger and more dignified. The clothes hanging awkwardly on hooks along the wall drew back into the shadows. All the light from the fire and from the open doorway fell on the gleaming white party table, waiting for General Washington.

"It's more beautiful than any table we ever set in Gettysburg," Ann whispered.

Mrs. Hamilton looked up from the hearth and smiled.

Later the table looked even more wonderful, piled high with steaming food—hot yellow corn bread, round bowls of green peas, roasted brown potatoes, a platter of cold venison, bowls of purple grape jelly, golden pumpkin pies. It was the same meal that they had had nearly every evening all summer on Hamilton Hill, but tonight with the lavender flowered plates, it managed to look different.

"I hope I look different too," Ann thought as she fingered her two blue hair ribbons and hastily tied the sash of a fresh apron.

She felt different. General Washington and Mr. Hamilton led the others into the cabin, and suddenly Ann found herself feeling strangely shy. All the time they were taking their places at the table, she kept her eyes down. It was not until her father was asking the blessing that she stole her first look up from under half-closed eyelashes. When she saw George Washington's head bowed over the white tablecloth and lavender plate, the peas and potatoes, Ann thought she could hardly bear her happiness.

During the rest of the meal, Ann followed the conversation in a kind of daze. She didn't seem to hear anything that anyone said, except General Washington. Everything he said rang out clear, with a special meaning, it almost seemed, just for her.

"If I were a young man," General Washington said, "preparing to begin the world, I know of no country where I should rather live."

"I am determined to find a way," he said again, "that we can join the waters of the West with those of the East so that the two countries may be close together."

Ann held onto every word, turned them over in her mind, locked them away in her heart. It was after the evening meal, after all the thank-you's had been said and General Washington and his party were preparing to leave that he said what Ann was to treasure forever afterward. He stood at the doorway, looking toward the west, his eyes resting on Hamilton Hill, yet somehow going beyond.

"The future is traveling west with people like you," he said to Mr. Hamilton. "Here is the rising world—to be kept or lost in the same way a battlefield is kept or lost."

General Washington turned to Ann and put his hand gently on her shoulder. "Through the courage of young girls as much as anyone's. You will live to see this whole country a rolling farmland, bright with houses and barns and churches. Some day. I envy you, Miss Hamilton."

That night, in the home of a Colonel Cannon several miles west of Hamilton Hill, before he blew out his candle, General George Washington sat down at a table and wrote this in his diary:

"September 18, 1784. Set out with Doctr. Craik for my Land on Miller's Run, crossed the Monongahela at Devore's Ferry . . . bated at one Hamilton's about 4 miles from it, in Washington County, and lodged at Colo. Cannon's."

That night in the cabin on Hamilton Hill, Ann took down from her shelf her deerskin-covered diary. Her heart was too full to write all she wanted. Instead she wrote in big letters across a whole page:

## *On the Move*

In *On the Move*, you read about people who lived long ago when our country was very young. Most of the characters faced great challenges and learned something from their experiences.

**Thinking About *On the Move***

1. Tell why the people in "The Courage of Sarah Noble," "Felipe and Filomena," "The White Stallion," "Wagon Wheels," and "The Town That Moved" decided to move. How were these stories different? How were they alike?

2. Name the stories in which an animal was important. Explain how the animals helped the people in the stories.

3. Paul Bunyan moved around our country. Tell about his travels and what he did in each spot.

4. If you were going to move to another part of the country, how would you get there? Why wouldn't you be able to move the way Gretchen's family did in "The White Stallion"?

5. One of the hardships that many of the people faced in *On the Move* was sleeping out in the cold. There were many others. Write about the other hardships the characters had to face.

# Glossary

This glossary can help you to pronounce and find out the meanings of words in this book that you may not know.

The words are listed in alphabetical order. Guide words at the top of each page tell you the first and last words on the page.

Each word is divided into syllables. The way to pronounce each word is given next. You can understand the pronunciation respelling by using the key below. A shorter key appears at the bottom of every other page.

When a word has more than one syllable, a dark accent mark (′) shows which syllable is stressed. In some words, a light accent mark (′) shows which syllable has a less heavy stress.

The following abbreviations are used in this glossary:

*n.* noun    *v.* verb    *adj.* adjective    *adv.* adverb    *pl.* plural
*conj.* conjunction

Glossary entries are adapted from the Macmillan *Beginning Dictionary*.

## PRONUNCIATION KEY

### Vowel Sounds

/a/ bat
/ā/ cake, rain, day
/ä/ father
/är/ car
/ãr/ dare, hair
/e/ hen, bread
/ē/ me, meat, baby, believe
/èr/ term, first, worm, turn

/i/ bib
/ī/ kite, fly, pie, light
/ir/ clear, cheer, here
/o/ top, watch
/ō/ rope, soap, so, snow
/ô/ saw, song, auto
/oi/ coin, boy
/ôr/ fork, ore, oar

/ou/ out, cow
/u/ sun, son, touch
/ù/ book, pull, could
/ü/ moon
/ū/ cute, few, music
/ə/ about, taken, pencil, apron, helpful
/ər/ letter, dollar, doctor

### Consonant Sounds

/b/ bear
/d/ dog
/f/ fish, phone
/g/ goat
/h/ house, who
/j/ jar, gem, fudge
/k/ car, key
/l/ lamb

/m/ map
/n/ nest, know
/p/ pig
/r/ rug, wrong
/s/ city, seal
/t/ tiger
/v/ van
/w/ wagon

/y/ yo-yo
/z/ zoo, eggs
/ch/ chain, match
/sh/ show
/th/ thin
/th/ those
/hw/ where
/ng/ song

329

# A

**ac·tiv·i·ties** (ak tiv′ə tēs) *n. sing.*,
**ac·tiv·i·ty.** things to do or be
done.

**al·li·ga·tors** (al′ə gā′ tərz) *n.*
animals with a long head and tail
and a thick, tough skin. They live
in rivers and marshes in America
and China. Alligators look like
crocodiles but have shorter,
wider heads.

**al·pha·bet** (al′ fə bet′) *n.* the
letters or symbols that are used
to write a language.

**al·though** (ôl thō′) *conj.* in spite of
the fact that; even though;
though.

**an·nounced** (ə nounsd′) *v.* made
something known.

**an·noyed** (ə noid′) *v.* bothered or
disturbed.

**an·nu·al** (an′ ū əl) *adj.* happening
once a year; yearly.

**an·te·lope** (ant′ əl ōp′) *n. pl.*,
**an·te·lope** or **an·te·lopes.** a
slender, swift animal that has long
horns. An antelope looks like a
deer, but it is related to the goat.

**An·za, Juan Bau·tis·ta de**
(än′ sä, hwän′ bou tēs′ tä dä)
1735–1788, Spanish explorer
and governor in North America;
founded the cities of Monterey
and San Francisco.

**A·pach·e** (ə pach′ ē) *n. pl.*,
**A·pach·e** or **A·pach·es.** a North
American Indian tribe living in
the southwestern United States.
*adj.* of or having to do with the
Apaches.

**ap·pre·ci·ate** (ə prē′ shē āt′) *v.*,
**ap·pre·ci·at·ed, ap·pre·ci·at
·ing. 1.** to recognize the value of
something. **2.** to be grateful for
something.

**Armstrong, Neil** (ärm′ strong′, nēl′)
the first American astronaut to
walk on the moon in 1969.

**ar·range·ment** (ə rānj′ mənt) *n.*
**1.** the act of putting in order.
**2.** something put in order.

**ar·ti·cle** (är′ ti kəl) *n.* **1.** a
composition written for a
newspaper, magazine, or book.
**2.** a particular thing or object; item.

**art·ist** (är′ tist) *n.* a person who
is skilled in painting, music,
literature, or any other form of art.

**as·sem·bly** (ə sem′ blē) *n. pl.*,
**as·sem·blies.** a group of people
gathered together for some
purpose.

**as·sist·ants** (ə sis′ tənts) *n.* people who help.

**as·ton·ished** (əs ton′ isht) *v.* surprised very much; amazed.

**at·tack** (ə tak′) *n.* the act of attacking. *v.* to begin to fight against.

**au·thors** (ô′ thərs) *n.* people who write books, stories, plays, poems, or articles.

**av·er·age** (av′ rij, av′ ər ij) *n.* **1.** the number found by dividing the sum of two or more quantities by the number of quantities. **2.** the usual amount or kind.

**ax·le** (ak′ səl) *n.* a bar or shaft on which a wheel or a pair of wheels turn.

# B

**ba·con** (bā′ kən) *n.* meat from the back and sides of a pig. Bacon is flavored with salt and treated with smoke to preserve it.

**bal·co·ny** (bal′ kə nē) *n. pl.*, **bal·co·nies.** a platform that juts out from the wall of a building. A balcony has a low wall or railing on three sides.

**ban·dan·na** (ban dan′ ə) *also,* **ban·dan·a.** *n.* a large handkerchief with a brightly colored pattern on it.

**ban·jo** (ban′ jō) *n. pl.*, **ban·jos** or **ban·joes.** a musical instrument that has a round body, a long neck, and five strings.

**bar·gain** (bär′ gin) *n.* **1.** an agreement. **2.** something offered for sale or bought at a low price. *v.* to try to reach a bargain.

**bar·rel** (bãr′ əl) *n.* a large, round wooden container with curved sides.

**base·ments** (bās′ mənts) *n.* the lowest floors of buildings.

**ba·tik** (bə tēk′) *n.* **1.** a method of hand printing colored designs on cloth or other things by putting a wax coating on the parts that are not to be dyed. **2.** cloth decorated by this method.

**be·hav·ior** (bi hāv′ yər) *n.* a way of behaving or acting.

---

a **bat**, ā **cake**, ä **father**, är **car**, ãr **dare**; e **hen**, ē **me**, ėr **term**; i **bib**, ī **kite**, ir **clear**; o **top**, ō **rope**, ô **saw**, oi **coin**, ôr **fork**, ou **out**; u **sun**, ů **book**, ü **moon**, ū **cute**; ə **about**, **taken**

**be·liefs** (bi lēfs') *n.* things that are believed to be true.

**birch** (bėrch) *n.* a tree that has hard wood and white bark that peels off in strips.

**boul·der** (bōl' dər) *n.* a large rock that is rounded and smooth.

**breed·er** (brē' dər) *n.* a person who raises plants or animals.

**bril·liant** (bril' yənt) *adj.* **1.** very bright; sparkling. **2.** very intelligent.

**buf·fa·loes** (buf'ə lōz') *also,* **buf·fa·los** or **buf·fa·lo.** *n. sing.,* **buf·fa·lo.** North American wild oxen; bison. Buffaloes have a big shaggy head with short horns and a humped back.

**bunk·house** (bungk' hous') *n. pl.,* **bunk·hous·es.** a building with sleeping quarters or bunks for workers or campers.

**bur·ro** (bėr' ō) *n. pl.,* **bur·ros.** a small donkey. Burros are used for riding and for carrying loads.

**buz·zards** (buz' ərdz) *n.* very large birds that have a sharp, hooked beak and long, sharp claws. A buzzard is a kind of hawk. Buzzards are birds of prey.

# C

**cab·bag·es** (kab' ij əs) *n.* plants that have thick green or reddish-purple leaves that form a round head. The leaves of the cabbage are eaten as a vegetable.

**camp·fires** (camp' fīrz') *n.* outdoor fires that are used for cooking or keeping warm in a camp.

**Can·a·da** (kan'ə də) *n.* the country north of the United States.

**ca·nar·y** (kə nãr' ē) *n. pl.,* **ca·nar·ies.** a small yellow songbird. Canaries are often kept as pets.

**can·vas** (kan' vəs) *n. pl.,* **can·va·ses.** a strong, heavy cloth made of cotton, flax, or hemp. Oil paintings are painted on pieces of canvas.

**can·yon** (kan' yən) *n.* a deep valley with very high, steep sides. A canyon often has a stream running through it.

**car·a·van** (kãr'ə van') *n.* a group of people who travel together.

**car·pen·ter** (kär' pən tər) *n.* a person who builds and repairs houses and other things made of wood.

**car·ri·er** (kãr′ ē ər) *n.* a person or thing that carries something.

**cat·a·logue** (kat′ əl ôg′, kat′ əl og′) *also,* **cat·a·log.** *n.* **1.** a list of books, names, subjects, or other items, that often identifies and describes each item. **2.** a book or other publication containing such a list.

**cause** (kôz) *n.* **1.** something a person or group believes in. **2.** a person or thing that makes something happen. *v.* **caused, caus·ing.** to make something happen; result in.

**ceil·ing** (sē′ ling) *n.* the inside covering above a room.

**cell** (sel) *n.* a unit.

**cham·pi·on** (cham′ pē ən) *n.* a person or thing that is the winner of first place in a contest or game.

**chaps** (chaps, shaps) *n. pl.,* strong leather coverings worn over trousers. Chaps are sometimes worn by cowboys to protect their legs while riding horses.

**char·i·ot** (char′ ē ət) *n.* a two-wheeled vehicle drawn by horses.

**chil·i** (chil′ ē) *also,* **chil·e, chil·li.** *n. pl.,* **chil·ies.** the dried pod of a plant, used to make a hot spice. The dish made of this spice, meat, tomato sauce, and beans—**chili con carne**—is often called **chili** for short.

**chow** (chou) *n.* slang for *food.*

**Clark, Wil·liam** (klärk′, wil′yəm) 1770–1838, an explorer who led an expedition to the Pacific Northwest with Meriwether Lewis.

**cloak** (klōk) *n.* a loose outer piece of clothing, with or without sleeves.

**clum·sy** (klum′ zē) *adj.* awkward, not graceful.

**coarse** (kôrs) *adj.* **1.** thick and rough. **2.** made up of rather large parts; not fine.

**cof·fin** (kô′ fin) *n.* a box in which a dead person is put to be buried.

**col·lapse** (kə laps′) *v.,* **col·lapsed, col·laps·ing.** to fail or break down completely or suddenly.

---

a bat, ā cake, ä father, är car, ãr dare; e hen, ē me, ėr term; i bib, ī kite, ir clear; o top, ō rope, ô saw, oi coin, ôr fork, ou out; u sun, u̇ book, ü moon, ū cute; ə about, taken

**col·o·ny** (kol′ə nē) *n. pl.,*
**col·o·nies. 1.** a territory that is
far away from the country that
governs it. **2.** a group of people
who leave their own country and
settle in another land.

**com·fort·a·ble** (kum′ fər tə bəl,
kumf′ tə bəl) *adj.* **1.** giving ease
or comfort. **2.** at ease.

**com·mand·ed** (kə man′ did) *v.*
gave an order to; directed.

**com·mu·ni·ca·tion** (kə mū′ ni ḳā′
shən) *n.* an exchanging of
information or thoughts.

**com·mu·ni·ty** (kə mū′ nə tē) *n. pl.,*
**com·mu·ni·ties.** a group of
people who live together in the
same place.

**com·pared** (kəm pärd′) *v.* studied
or found out how persons or
things are alike or different.

**com·pete** (kəm pēt′) *v.* **com·pet
·ed, com·pet·ing.** to try to win
or gain something from another
or others.

**com·plain** (kəm plān′) *v.* to say that
something is wrong; find fault.

**com·pos·er** (kəm pō′ zər) *n.* a
person who composes a musical
work or anything else.

**Con·es·to·ga wag·on** (kon′ is tō′
gə wag′ ən) *n.* a covered wagon
with an arched canvas top and
broad wheels, used by the

pioneers to cross the American
prairies.

**con·fuse** (kən′ fūz) *v.* **con·fused,
con·fus·ing.** to mix up; bewilder.

**con·fu·sion** (kən fū′ zhən) *n.*
**1.** disorder or bewilderment.
**2.** a mistaking of a person or
thing for another.

**con·tain·er** (kən tā′ nər) *n.* a box,
can, or jar that holds something.

**con·ti·nent** (kont′ ən ənt) *n.* one of
the seven large land areas on the
earth. The continents are Asia,
Africa, North America, South
America, Antarctica, Europe, and
Australia.

**Con·ti·nen·tal Con·gress** (kon′ tə
nent′ əl   kong′ gris) *n.* the
assembly of delegates from the
American colonies that met from
1774 to 1781.

**con·tin·ued** (kən tin′ ūd) *v.* kept on
happening; went on.

**con·trol** (kən trōl′) *n.* power or
authority. *v.,* **con·trol,
con·trol·ling.** to have power or
authority over.

**con·ver·sa·tion** (kon′ vər sā′ shən)
*n.* a friendly and informal talk.

**corn·meal** (kôrn′ mēl′) *also,* **corn meal.** *n.* meal made from coarsely ground corn.

**cor·ri·dor** (kôr′ə dər) *n.* a long hallway or passageway in a building.

**coun·cil** (koun′ səl) *n.* a group of people called together. A <u>council</u> can give advice, discuss a problem, or make a decision.

**cour·age** (kėr′ ij) *n.* a strength that a person has that helps him or her to face danger by overcoming fear.

**court·yard** (kôrt′ yärd′) *n.* an open area that is surrounded by walls or buildings.

**cranes** (krānz) *n.* large machines with a long arm that can be moved up and down and in a circle. Cranes are used to lift and move heavy objects that are attached to cables at the end of the arm.

**cro·cus·es** (krō′ kəs əs) *also* **cro·ci** (kro′ si) *n. sing.,* **cro·cus** (kro′ kəs) small flowers that grow from underground bulbs. <u>Crocuses</u> grow in many colors and have thin leaves like blades of grass. They are one of the first flowers to bloom in the spring.

**cul·tures** (kul′ chərz) *n.* the arts, beliefs, and customs that make up the ways of life for different groups of people at certain times.

**cu·ri·ous** (kyür′ ē əs) *adj.* eager to learn about things that are new, strange, or interesting.

**cur·tain** (kėr′ tin) *n.* **1.** a piece of cloth or other material hung across an open space such as a window or door. **2.** anything that screens or covers like a curtain.

**cus·toms** (kus′ təmz) *n.* ways of acting that have become accepted by many people. <u>Customs</u> are learned and passed down from one generation to another.

---

a bat, ā cake, ä father, är car, ãr dare; e hen, ē me, ėr term; i bib, ī kite; ir clear; o top, ō rope, ô saw, oi coin, ôr fork, ou out; u sun, u̇ book, ü moon, ū cute; ə about, taken

**cy·clone** (sī′ klōn) *n.* a very powerful windstorm.

# D

**dai·ly** (dā′ lē) *adj.* appearing, done, or happening every day or every weekday. *adv.* day after day; every day.

**de·feat** (di fēt′) *n.* the state of being defeated in a contest of any kind. *v.* to win a victory over; overcome in a contest of any kind.

**def·i·nite·ly** (def′ə nit lē) *adv.* in a certain or clear manner.

**de·li·cious** (di lish′ əs) *adj.* pleasing or delightful to the taste or smell.

**de·liv·er·y** (di liv′ ər ē) *n. pl.,* **de·liv·er·ies.** the act of carrying or taking something to a place or person.

**de·signs** (di zīnz′) *n.* arrangements of different parts or colors; patterns. *v.* makes a plan, drawing, or outline of; makes a pattern for.

**de·tec·tive** (di tek′ tiv) *n.* a person who searches for information to solve a crime and finds the one who committed it. *adj.* having to do with detectives and their work.

**dis·cour·aged** (dis kėr′ ijd) *v.* caused to lose courage, hope, or confidence.

**dis·grace** (dis grās′) *n.* the loss of honor or respect. *v.,* **dis·graced, dis·grac·ing.** to bring shame to.

**dis·tance** (dis′ təns) *n.* **1.** a far-off point or place. **2.** the amount of space between two things or points.

**dis·tant** (dis′ tənt) *adj.* far away in space or time; not near.

**dis·tress** (dis tres′) *n.* great pain or sorrow; misery.

**dug·out** (dug′ out′) *n.* a rough shelter that is made by digging a hole in the ground or in the side of a hill.

**du·ra·ble** (dür′ə bəl, dyur′ə bəl) *adj.* able to last a long time in spite of much use or wear.

**du·ty** (dü′ tē, dū′ tē) *n. pl.,* **du·ties.** something that a person is supposed to do.

# E

**ea·ger·ness** (ē′ gər nis) *n.* a strong desire; the state of wanting very much to do something.

**egg-dye·ing** (eg′ dī′ ing) *n.* the act or process of coloring eggs with dye.

**elk** (elk) *n. pl.,* **elk** or **elks.** a large deer of North America. The male elk has very large antlers.

**em·broi·der·y** (em broi′ dər ē) *n. pl.,* **em·broi·der·ies.** designs that have been sewn on cloth with thread.

**en·e·my** (en′ə mē) *n. pl.,* **en·e ·mies.** a person or animal that wishes to harm another.

**Eng·land** (ing′ glənd) *n.* the largest part of the island of Great Britain, in the southern part.

**e·nor·mous** (i nôr′ məs) *adj.* much greater than the usual size or amount; very large.

**e·ven·tu·al·ly** (i ven′ chü ə lē) *adv.* in the end; finally.

**ex·act·ly** (eg zakt′ lē) *adv.* precisely; in an exact manner; accurately.

**ex·cel·lent** (ek′ sə lənt) *adj.* very, véry good; outstanding.

**ex·change** (eks chānj′) *v.* **ex·changed, ex·chang·ing.** to give up for something else; change.

**ex·claimed** (eks clāmd′) *v.* spoke or cried out suddenly.

**ex·per·i·ment** (*n.,* eks pãr′ ə mənt; *v.,* eks pãr′ ə ment′) *n.* a test that is used to discover or prove something. *v.* to make an experiment or experiments.

**ex·pert** (eks′ pėrt) *n.* a person who knows a great deal about some special thing.

**ex·plode** (eks plōd′) *v.* **ex·plod·ed, ex·plod·ing. 1.** to burst forth suddenly and with a loud noise; blow up. **2.** to break forth noisily or with force.

# F

**faith·ful·ly** (fāth′ fəl ē) *adv.* in a loyal and devoted way.

**fa·mous** (fā′ məs) *adj.* very well known.

**fan·cy** (fan′ sē) *adj.* not plain; highly decorated.

**fas·ten·ing** (fas′ ə ning) *v.* attaching, closing, or putting firmly.

---

a bat, ā cake, ä father, är car, ãr dare; e hen, ē me, ėr term; i bib, ī kite, ir clear; o top, ō rope, ô saw, oi coin, ôr fork, ou out; u sun, ù book, ü moon, ū cute; ə about, taken

**fe·male** (fē′ māl) *adj.* of or having to do with the sex that gives birth to young or produces eggs. *n.* a female person or animal.

**fer·ry·boat** (fãr′ ē bōt′) *n.* a boat used to carry people, cars, and goods across a river or other narrow body of water.

**fierce** (fērs) *adj.* **1.** cruel or dangerous; savage. **2.** very strong or violent; raging.

**fi·nal·ists** (fīn′ əl ists) *n.* people who take part in the final match or event of a series of games or contests.

**firm·er** (fėrm′ ər) *adj.* more steady or stronger.

**fish·er·man** (fish′ ər mən) *n.* a person who fishes for a living or for sport.

**flap·jacks** (flap′ jaks′) *n.* flat, thin cakes made of batter and cooked in a pan or on a griddle; pancakes.

**flax** (flaks) *n.* a fiber that comes from the stem of a certain plant.

**flum·ma·did·dle** (flum′ə did′ əl) *n.* nonsense.

**folk·lore** (fōk′ lôr′) *n.* the tales, beliefs, customs, or other traditions of a people, handed down from generation to generation.

**folks** (fōks) *n.* people.

**foo-foo** (fü′ fü) *n.* a word used to mean <u>food</u> among some West African peoples.

**for·tunes** (fôr′ chəns) *n.* **1.** great wealth; riches. **2.** things good or bad that will happen to people.

**fowls** (fouls) *also,* **fowl.** *n. sing.,* **fowl. 1.** birds that are used for food. **2.** birds in general.

**fra·grant** (frā′ grənt) *adj.* having a sweet or pleasing smell.

**France** (frans) *n.* a country in western Europe.

**fruit** (früt) *n. pl.,* **fruit** or **fruits.** the part of a plant that contains the seeds.

**fur·ni·ture** (fėr′ ni chər) *n.* tables, chairs, beds, and other removeable articles used in a home or office.

# G

**Ger·ma·ny** (jėr′ mə nē) *n.* a country in northcentral Europe.

**Gha·na** (gä′ nə) *n.* a country in West Africa.

**ghost** (gōst) *n.* the supposed spirit of a dead person.

**Gi·la mon·sters** (hē′ lə mon′ stərz) *n.* large, poisonous lizards found in desert regions of the southwestern United States and northern Mexico.

**go·ril·la** (gə ril′ ə) *n.* a large, very strong animal that is a kind of monkey. Gorillas have big, heavy bodies, short legs, and long arms. They live in Africa.

**gov·ern·ment** (guv′ ərn mənt, guv′ ər mənt) *n.* the group of people in charge of ruling or managing a country, state, city, or other place.

**griz·zly** (griz′ lē) *n. pl.,* **griz·zlies.** a grizzly bear. A grizzly bear is a very large, powerful bear. It has long claws and usually brown or gray fur. Grizzly bears live in western North America.

**guide** (gīd) *n.* a person or thing that shows the way or directs.

# H

**har·bor** (här′ bər) *n.* a sheltered place along a coast. Ships and boats often anchor in a harbor.

**hard·ships** (härd′ ships′) *n.* things that cause difficulty, pain, or suffering.

**har·ness** (här′ nis) *n. pl.,* **har·ness ·es.** the straps, bands, and other fastenings used to attach a work animal to a cart, plow, or wagon.

**head·quar·ters** (hed′ kwôr′ tərz) *n. pl.* any center of operations or business.

**heav·ens** (hev′ ənz) *n.* the space above and around the earth; sky. The word **heavens** is sometimes used as an exclamation to express surprise or amazement.

**herd** (hėrd) *n.* a group of animals.

**hes·i·tant·ly** (hez′ ət ənt lē) *adv.* in a doubtful or uncertain manner.

**Hib·bing, Frank** (hib′ ing, frangk′) the man who founded the town of Hibbing in Minnesota.

a bat, ā cake, ä father, är car, âr dare; e hen, ē me, ėr term; i bib, ī kite, ir clear; o top, ō rope, ô saw, oi coin, ôr fork, ou out; u sun, ů book, ü moon, ū cute; ə about, taken

**hic·cups** (hik′ ups) *also,*
**hic·coughs.** *n.* quick catchings of
the breath that one cannot
control.

**hinged** (hinjd) *adj.* attached by
hinges. A hinge is a jointed piece
on which a door, gate, or lid
moves back and forth or up and
down.

**his·to·ry** (his′ tər ē) *n. pl.,*
**his·to·ries.** the story or record
of what has happened in the past.

**hog·wash** (hog′ wosh′, hog′
wôsh′) *n.* worthless or
nonsensical talk or writing.

**Home·stead Act** (hōm′ sted′ akt′)
a law passed by the United
States Congress in 1862 to
distribute public land to settlers
for farming.

**hon·ey** (hun′ ē) *n.* a thick, sweet
liquid made by bees. Bees collect
nectar from flowers and make
honey, which they store in
honeycombs.

**hon·ey·combs** (hun′ ē kōmz′) *n.*
wax structures made by bees to
store their honey in.

**hon·ored** (on′ ərd) *v.* given honor
to; favored; dignified.

**hooves** (húvz, hüvz) *n. sing.,* **hoof.**
the hard coverings on the feet of
horses, cattle, deer, and certain
other animals.

**Hu·mane So·ci·e·ty** (hū mān′
sə sī′ə tē) *n.* a group of people
concerned with kind and proper
treatment of animals.

# I

**ig·nore** (ig nôr′) *v.* **ig·nored, ig·nor
·ing.** to pay no attention to.

**i·gua·na** (i gwä′ nə) *n.* a large
greenish-brown lizard. It is found
in the very warm parts of
America. The iguana lives in trees.

**im·pos·si·ble** (im pos′ə bəl) *adj.*
not able to happen or be done.

**in·de·pend·ence** (in′ di pen′ dəns)
*n.* freedom from the control of
another or others.

**in·stant** (in′ stənt) *adj.* without
delay; immediate. *n.* a very short
period of time; moment.

**in·tel·li·gent** (in tel′ə jənt) *adj.*
having or showing intelligence;
bright.

**in·tro·duce** (in′ trə düs′, in′ trə
düs′) *v.,* **in·tro·duced, in·tro
·duc·ing.** to make known or
acquainted.

**Ire·land** (īr′ lənd) *n.* a large island
west of England. Ireland is one of
the British Isles.

**i·ron ore** (ī' ərn  ôr') *n.* rock found in the earth containing enough iron to make mining it worthwhile. <u>Iron</u> is a greyish-white metal used in making steel.

# J

**Jef·fer·son, Pres·i·dent** (jef' ər sən, prez' ə dənt) 1743–1826, Thomas Jefferson, who was the third president, or head of the government, of the United States, from 1801 to 1809

**jer·sey** (jèr'zē) *n.* **1.** a cloth that is knitted by machine out of wool, cotton, or other materials. <u>Jersey</u> is very soft and is used to make clothing. **2.** a sweater made out of this cloth. It is put on over the head.

**john·ny·cake** (jon' ē  kāk') *n.* a flat, crisp bread made of cornmeal, water or milk, flour, and sometimes, eggs. It is often baked in a pan or on a griddle.

**jour·ney** (jèr' nē) *n.* a long trip. *v.* to make a trip; travel.

# K

**kan·ga·roo** (kang' gə rü') *n. pl.*, **kan·ga·roos** or **kan·ga·roo.** an Australian animal that has small front legs and very strong back legs that it uses for leaping. A kangaroo also has a long powerful tail that is used for balance. A female <u>kangaroo</u> carries her young in a pouch for about six months after birth.

**Kos·ci·us·ko, Thad·de·us** (kos' ē us' kō,  thad' ē əs) 1746–1817, a Polish patriot and commander of American troops in the Revolutionary War.

# L

**land·marks** (land' märks') *n.* objects that are familiar and serve as guides.

**lan·terns** (lan' tərns) *n.* coverings for lights. Some lanterns are made of metal with sides of glass. Most <u>lanterns</u> can be carried.

---

a bat, ā cake, ä father, är **car**, ãr **dare**; e hen, ē me, ėr **term**; i bib, ī **kite**, ir **clear**; o top, ō rope, ô saw, oi coin, ôr fork, ou out; u sun, u̇ book, ü moon, ū cute; ə about, taken

**la·ser beams** (lā' zər bēmz') *n.* very strong beams, or rays, of light produced by a device called a laser.

**law** (lô) *n.* any rule.

**leath·er** (leth' ər) *n.* a material made from an animal skin that has been tanned.

**Lew·is, Mer·i·weth·er** (lü' is, mãr' ē weth' ər) 1774–1809, an American explorer who led an expedition to the Pacific Northwest with William Clark.

**lin·en** (lin' ən) *n.* a strong cloth woven from fibers of flax.

**lo·ca·tions** (lō kā' shəns) *n.* places where things are located; sites.

**log·ger** (lô' gər, log' ər) *n.* a person who chops down trees in a forest and cuts them into logs.

**loom** (lüm) *n.* a machine for weaving thread into cloth.

**loud·speak·er** (loud' spē' kər) *n.* a device that can change electrical signals into sounds and make the sounds louder.

**lum·ber·jacks** (lum' bər jaks') *n.* people who cut down trees and get logs ready for the sawmill.

# M

**mag·nif·i·cent** (mag nif'ə sənt) *adj.* quite beautiful and grand; splendid.

**ma·jor** (mā' jər) *adj.* bigger or more important.

**man·kind** (man' kīnd') *n.* the human race; all people.

**Manx** (mangks) *adj.* having to do with the Isle of Man. The famous tailless cat from the Isle of Man is called the Manx cat.

**mare** (mãr) *n.* the female of the horse, donkey, zebra, or certain other animals.

**mead·ow** (med' ō) *n.* a field of grassy land. It is often used for growing hay or as a pasture for animals.

**meas·ured** (mezh' ərd) *v.* had as a measurement.

**med·i·cine man** (med' ə sin man') *n.* a person in certain North American Indian tribes who was believed to have magic powers.

**mer·maid** (mer' mād') *n.* an imaginary creature that was believed to live in the sea. It had the head and body of a beautiful woman and the tail of a fish.

**mi·cro·phones** (mī' krə fōnz') *n.* devices that are used to transmit sound or to make it louder.

**mir·a·cle** (mir'ə kəl) *n.* **1.** an amazing or wonderful thing. **2.** something amazing or wonderful that cannot be explained by the laws of nature.

**mis·sion** (mish' ən) *n.* a church or other place used by missionaries in their work.

**mod·ern** (mod' ərn) *adj.* having to do with the present time or recent time.

**mo·las·ses** (mə las' iz) *n.* a sweet, thick, yellowish-brown syrup that is made from sugarcane.

**moon·shine** (mün' shīn') *n.* empty talk or ideas; nonsense.

**moose** (müs) *n. pl.,* **moose.** a large, heavy animal related to the deer that lives in forests in the northern United States and Canada. The male moose has enormous, broad antlers.

**mos·qui·to** (məs kē' tō) *n. pl.,* **mos·qui·toes** or **mos·qui·tos.** a small insect with two wings. The female gives a sharp sting or bite that itches.

**muf·fler** (muf' lər) *n.* a warm scarf that is wrapped around the neck in cold weather.

**mus·cles** (mus' əls) *n.* tissues in the body of a person or animal, that are made up of strong fibers. Muscles can be tightened or relaxed to make the body move. Our muscles give us strength to lift and carry.

**mus·ket** (mus' kit) *n.* a gun with a long barrel like a rifle. Muskets were used in warfare before modern rifles were invented.

**mus·tangs** (mus' tangz) *n.* wild horses that live on the Mexican plains.

# N

**nar·ra·tor** (nar' ā tər, na rā' tər, nar'ə tər) *also,* **nar·ra·ter.** *n.* one who tells or gives an oral or written account of; one who tells a story.

---

a bat, ā cake, ä father, är car, ãr dare; e hen, ē me, ėr term; i bib, ī kite, ir clear; o top, ō rope, ô saw, oi coin, ôr fork, ou out; u sun, ủ book, ü moon, ū cute; ə about, taken

**na·tion** (nā′ shən) *n.* a particular land where a group of people live together under one government and share the same language, culture, and history.

**nat·u·ral·ly** (nach′ ər ə lē) *adv.* as would be expected; of course.

**na·ture** (nā′ chər) *n.* the physical universe; all the things that are not made by people. The mountains, forests, and oceans are parts of <u>nature</u>.

**nuz·zled** (nuz′ əld) *v.* touched or rubbed with the nose.

# O

**o·bey** (ō bā′) *v.* to carry out the orders, wishes, or instructions of.

**ob·jects** (*n.*, ob′ jikts; *v.*, əb jekts′) *n.* things that can be seen and touched; things. *v.* being against; having or raising an objection.

**of·fi·cer** (ô′ fə sər) *n.* **1.** a person who has the power to command and lead others in the army or navy. Captains, generals, and admirals are officers. **2.** a person who has a position of authority, trust, or responsibility. The president and vice-president of a company are <u>officers</u>.

**op·po·site** (op′ ə zit) *n.* a person or thing that is completely different from another. *adj.* completely different.

**o·rig·i·nal** (ə rij′ ən əl) *adj.* that has not been made, done, thought of, or used before; new.

**O·sage** (ō′ sāj, ō sāj′) *n.* a tribe of North American Indians, originally living in parts of Kansas, Missouri, and Illinois, now living in Oklahoma. *adj.* of or having to do with the Osage.

**ot·ter** (ot′ ər) *n. pl.*, **ot·ters** or **ot·ter.** a water animal that looks like a weasel.

**owl·et** (ou′ lit) *n.* a young or small owl.

# P

**pan·el** (pan′ əl) *n.* a group of persons gathered together to talk about or judge something.

**pan·el·ists** (pan′ əl ists) *n.* people who serve on a panel.

**pan·thers** (pan′ thərz) *n.* large leopards with a black coat.

**pa·rade** (pə rād′) *n.* a march or procession in honor of a person or an event.

**par·rot** (pãr′ ət) *n.* a bird with a wide curved bill, a long pointed tail, and glossy, brightly colored feathers. Some parrots can imitate speech and other sounds. <u>Parrots</u> are sometimes kept as pets.

**pars·ley** (pärs′ lē) *n.* a small plant that has many tiny leaves on each branch. It is used to flavor and decorate food.

**pa·tience** (pā′ shəns) *n.* being able to put up with hardship, pain, trouble, or delay without getting angry or upset.

**pa·tri·ot** (pā′ trē ət) *n.* a person who loves his or her country and defends or supports it with loyalty.

**per·fect** (pėr′ fikt) *adj.* without a mistake or fault.

**per·ma·nent** (pėr′ mə nənt) *adj.* lasting or meant to last; enduring.

**pi·geons** (pij′ əns) *n.* birds that have a plump body, a small head, and thick soft feathers.

**Pil·grims** (pil′ grəms) *n.* the English settlers who founded Plymouth, Massachusetts, the first permanent settlement in New England.

**Pi·ma** (pē′ mə) *n. pl.*, **Pi·ma** or **Pi·mas.** a tribe of North American Indians living in southern Arizona and northern Mexico. *adj.* of or having to do with the Pimas.

**pi·o·neers** (pī′ ə nērz′) *n.* people who are the first to explore and settle a region.

**pla·za** (plä′ zə, plaz′ə) *n. pl.*, **pla·zas.** a public square or open space in a city or town.

**plot·ting** (plot′ing) *v.* making a secret plan.

**plow** (plou) *v.* to turn over with a plow. *n.* a heavy farm tool for breaking up soil. A farmer uses a plow to prepare soil for planting seeds.

**po·si·tion** (pə zish′ ən) *n.* **1.** the place where a person or thing is. **2.** a way of being placed. *v.* to put in a particular place or arrangement.

**pos·si·ble** (pos′ ə bəl) *adj.* capable of being, being done, or happening.

**poul·try** (pōl′ trē) *n.* chickens, turkeys, geese, and other birds raised for their eggs or meat.

**poured** (pôrd) *v.* flowed or caused to flow.

---

a bat, ā cake, ä father, är **car**, är dare; e hen, ē me, ėr term; i bib, ī kite, ir clear; o top, ō rope, ô saw, oi coin, ôr fork, ou out; u sun, ù book, ü moon, ū cute; ə about, taken

**prai·rie** (prãr′ ē) *n.* flat or rolling land covered with grass.

**pranced** (pranst) *v.* moved in a proud, happy way.

**prob·lem** (prob′ ləm) *n.* a question or condition that is difficult to deal with or that has not been solved.

**pro·duced** (prə düsd′, prə düsd) *v.* made or created.

**pro·grams** (prō′ gramz) *n.* plays or other presentations or performances.

**pun·ish** (pun′ ish) *v.* to make a person suffer for a wrong he or she has done.

**py·thon** (pī′ thon) *n.* a large snake that coils around its prey and crushes or suffocates it.

# Q

**quar·rel** (kwôr′ əl) *n.* an angry argument or disagreement. *v.* to have an angry argument or disagreement.

# R

**rat·tle·snake** (rat′ əl snāk′) *n.* a poisonous American snake. A rattlesnake has a number of horny rings at the end of its tail that rattle when it shakes its tail.

**raw·hide** (rô′ hīd′) *n.* the hide of cattle or other animals that has not been tanned.

**re·fuse** (ri fūs′) *v.* **re·fused, re·fus·ing.** to say no to; reject.

**reins** (rānz) *n.* two or more narrow straps that are attached to a bridle or bit. Reins are used to guide and control a horse or other animal.

**re·plied** (ri plīd′) *v.* answered in speech, writing, or action.

**res·cues** (res′ kūz) *v.* saves or frees, as from danger.

**re·search** (ri sėrch′, re′sėrch′) *n. pl.,* **re·search·es.** a careful study or investigation in order to find and learn facts. *v.* to do research for.

**re·sem·ble** (ri zem′ bəl) *v.* **re·sem·bled, re·sem·bling.** to be like or similar to.

**re·spond** (ri spond′) *v.* **1.** to give an answer. **2.** to act in return; react.

**res·tau·rant** (res′ tər ənt) *n.* a place where food is prepared and served to customers at tables by a waiter or waitress.

**rest·less** (rest′ lis) *adj.* not able to rest.

**re·tired** (ri tīrd') *v.* taken oneself away from a business, job, or office.

**rou·tine** (rü tēn') *n.* a regular way of doing something.

**rule** (rül) *v.* **ruled, rul·ing.** to have power or control over; govern.

# S

**Sac·a·ja·we·a** (sak' ə jə wē'ə) 1788?–1812, an American Indian woman of the Shoshoni tribe who served as a guide and interpreter for the Lewis and Clark expedition.

**sad·dle·bag** (sad' əl bag') *n.* a bag of leather or other material, usually one of a pair that is hung from a saddle.

**sa·la·mi** (sə lä' mē) *n. pl.,* **sa·la·mis.** a sausage made of pork or beef and spices.

**sand·wich·es** (sand' wich əz) *n. sing.,* **sandwich.** two or more slices of bread with a filling of meat, cheese, or other food.

**sat·is·fy** (sat' is fī') *v.* **sat·is·fied, sat·is·fy·ing.** to meet the needs or desires of; to make contented.

**sau·sage** (sô' sij) *n.* finely chopped meat that is mixed with spices and stuffed into a thin case like a tube.

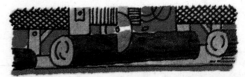

**saw·mill** (sô' mil') *n.* a place where machines saw logs into lumber.

**scarce·ly** (skãrs' lē) *adv.* barely or hardly.

**scars** (skärz) *n.* marks on the skin left by a cut or burn that has healed.

**scoured** (skourd) *v.* went or moved over or through, especially in making a thorough search.

**se·cure·ly** (si kyùr' lē) *adv.* in a stable, strong, or safe way.

**se·ñor** (sān yôr') *n. pl.,* **se·ño·res** (sān yôr' as). sir; mister. **Señor** is the Spanish form of address for a man.

**sep·a·rat·ed** (sep' ə rāt' id) *v.* set apart; placed apart.

**se·ries** (sēr' ēz) *n. pl.,* **se·ries.** a number of similar things coming one after another.

---

a **b**at, ā **c**ake, ä **f**ather, är **c**ar, ãr **d**are; e **h**en, ē **m**e, ėr **t**erm; i **b**ib, ī **k**ite; ir **cl**ear; o **t**op, ō **r**ope, ô **s**aw, oi **c**oin, ôr **f**ork, ou **o**ut; u **s**un, ù **b**ook, ü **m**oon, ū **c**ute; ə **a**bout, tak**e**n

**set·tle·ment** (set' əl mənt) *n.* **1.** a small village or group of houses. **2.** the act of settling or the condition of being settled.

**set·tlers** (set' lərz) *n.* people who settle in a new land or country.

**sew·ers** (sü' ərz) *n.* underground pipes or channels for carrying off waste water and refuse.

**shawl** (shôl) *n.* a piece of cloth that is worn over the shoulders or head.

**sheared** (shērd) *v.* cut or clipped with shears or scissors.

**shel·ter** (shel' tər) *n.* something that covers or protects.

**sher·iff** (sher' if) *n.* the main law officer of a county. The sheriff is in charge of keeping order and taking care of the jail.

**shift** (shift) *n.* **1.** a group of workers or the time that they work. **2.** a movement or change. *v.* to move or change.

**shin·gles** (shing' gəls) *n.* thin pieces of wood or other material. Shingles are placed in overlapping rows on roofs and sometimes on walls of buildings.

**Sho·sho·ni** (shə shō' nē, shō shō' nē) *also,* **Sho·sho·ne.** *n. pl.,* **Sho·sho·ni** or **Sho·sho·nis.** a tribe of North American Indians living in Idaho, Montana, Nevada, Oregon, Wyoming, and Utah. *adj.* of or having to do with the Shoshonis.

**shoul·ders** (shōl' dərz) *n.* the parts on either side of the body to which the arms are attached.

**sig·nal** (sig' nəl) *n.* something that warns, directs, or informs.

**so·lar sys·tem** (sō' lər sis' təm) *n.* the sun and all the planets, satellites, and comets that revolve around it.

**sol·diers** (sōl' jərz) *n.* people who are members of armies.

**sol·id** (sol' id) *adj.* very strong and reliable.

**so·lu·tion** (sə lü' shən) *n.* the answer to a problem.

**Spain** (spān) *n.* a country in southwestern Europe.

**spir·its** (spir' its) *n.* supernatural beings.

**sprawled** (sprôld) *v.* lay or sat with the body stretched out in an awkward or careless manner.

**spurs** (spurz) *n.* sharp metal pieces worn on the heels of a rider's boots. Spurs are used to make a horse go faster.

**spy·glass·es** (spī′ glas′ əz) *n. sing.*, **spy·glass.** binoculars; a device that makes distant objects look larger and closer. A <u>spyglass</u> is a small telescope.

**Squan·to** (skwon′ tō) d. 1622. a North American Indian of the Pawtuxet tribe who became friendly with the Pilgrims and helped them with their planting and fishing.

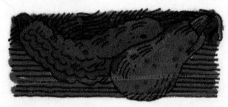

**squash** (skwosh) *n. pl.*, **squash·es.** any of several vegetables of various shapes that are usually yellow or green in color.

**stalked** (stôkt) *v.* **1.** walked in a stiff, proud manner. **2.** followed quietly and carefully so as to catch.

**stal·lion** (stal′ yən) *n.* a male horse.

**stam·pedes** (stam. pēdz′) *n.* sudden wild rushings of frightened herds of animals.

**starv·ing** (stär′ ving) *adj.* suffering from or dying of hunger.

**state** (stāt) *n.* a group of people living in a political unit that is part of a larger government.

**stead·y** (sted′ ē) *adj.* **1.** going at an even rate. **2.** not changing; regular. **3.** firm in movement or position; not shaky.

**Steu·ben, Bar·on von** (stü′ bən, stū′ bən  bār′ ən von) 1730–1794, German-born military leader who trained and organized the Continental Army under Washington. He became a naturalized American citizen in 1783.

**storks** (stôrks) *n.* birds with long legs, a long neck, and a long bill.

**strength** (strength) *n.* the quality of being strong; energy, power, or force.

**stretch** (strech) *n.* an unbroken space or area. *v.* to spread out one's arms, legs, or body to full length.

**stroll** (strōl) *n.* a slow relaxed walk. *v.* to walk in a slow, relaxed way.

**stud·ied** (stud′ ēd) *v.* tried to learn by reading or thinking about something.

---

a **bat**, ā **cake**, ä **father**, är **car**, ãr **dare**; e **hen**, ē **me**, ėr **term**; i **bib**, ī **kite**; ir **clear**; o **top**, ō **rope**, ô **saw**, oi **coin**, ôr **fork**, ou **out**; u **sun**, u̇ **book**, ü **moon**, ū **cute**; ə **about**, tak**e**n

**stu·di·o** (stü′ dē ō′, styü′ dē ō′) *n.* **1.** a place where radio or television programs are broadcast. **2.** a place where a painter or other artist works. **3.** a place where motion pictures are filmed.

**stum·bled** (stum′ bəld) *v.* lost one's balance; tripped.

**stu·pen·dous** (stü pen′ dəs, stū pen′ dəs) *adj.* causing amazement or astonishment; overwhelming.

**sub·ject** (sub′ jikt) *n.* **1.** something thought or talked about. **2.** a person or thing that is under the control of another.

**sub·way** (sub′ wā′) *n.* a railway that runs underground.

**sug·gest·ed** (səg jes′ tid) *v.* offered as something to think about.

**su·per·in·tend·ent** (sü′ pər in ten′ dənt) *n.* a person who directs or manages something.

**sup·plies** (sə plīz′) *n. sing.,* **sup·ply.** a quantity of something that is needed or ready for use. *v.* provides with something needed or wanted.

**sup·pose** (sə pōz′) *v.* **sup·posed,** **sup·pos·ing. 1.** imagine to be possible. **2.** to believe.

**swamp** (swomp) *n.* soft, wet land. Swamps have trees and shrubs growing in them.

**Swe·den** (swēd′ ən) *n.* a country in northern Europe.

**sym·bols** (sim′ bəlz) *n.* things that stand for or represent other things.

# T

**tape re·cord·er** (tāp′ ri kôr′ dər) *n.* a machine that records sound on a specially treated plastic tape. A tape recorder can then play back the sound that has been recorded.

**temp·ted** (temp′ tid) *v.* **1.** appealed strongly to; attracted. **2.** persuaded to do something that is wrong or foolish.

**ter·ri·fied** (tãr′ ə fīd′) *v.* filled with terror; frightened greatly.

**ter·ri·to·ry** (tãr′ ə tôr′ ē) *n. pl.,* **ter·ri·to·ries. 1.** any large area of land; region. **2.** land that is under the control of a distant government.

**the·a·ter** (thē′ ə tər) *also,* **the·a·tre.** *n.* a building or other place where plays or motion pictures are presented.

**trac·tors** (trak′ tərs) *n.* vehicles with heavy tires or a chain of continuous metal tracks. Tractors are used to pull heavy loads over rough ground.

**tribe** (trīb) *n.* a group of people who are joined because they have the same ancestors, social customs, and other characteristics.

**Trum·bull, Gov·er·nor** (trum' bəl, guv' ər nər) 1710–1785, Jonathan Trumbull, American statesman, Colonial governor of Connecticut from 1769 to 1784; supported the Revolutionary War.

**trum·pet·er swans** (trum' pit ər swonz') *n.* large white swans of western North America.

**tur·moil** (tur' moil) *n.* great confusion or disorder.

**tur·nips** (tėr' nips) *n.* round white or yellow vegetables that are the roots of certain plants.

**twit·tered** (twit' ərd) *v.* made short, light chirping sounds.

# U

**un·car·pet·ed** (un' kär' pi tid) *adj.* not covered or furnished with a carpet.

**un·der·neath** (un' dər nēth') *prep.* in a lower place or position than; on the underside of.

**ush·ers** (ush' ərs) *n.* people who lead other people to their seats in a church, theater, stadium, or other places. *v.* acts as an usher.

# V

**val·ley** (val' ē) *n.* an area of low land between hills or mountains.

**vice·roy** (vīs' roi') *n.* a governor of a province, kingdom, or colony, ruling with the authority of a king or other sovereign.

**vic·to·ries** (vik' tə rēz) *n. sing.,* **vic·to·ry.** defeats of an enemy or opponent.

**vid·e·o·tape** (vid' ē ō tāp') *n.* a magnetic tape used for recording both the picture and sound of a television program.

**view** (vū) *n.* **1.** the range or extent of seeing. **2.** the act of looking or seeing; sight. *v.* to look at or see.

**vi·nyl** (vin' əl) *n.* a kind of bendable, shiny plastic used for floor tiles, raincoats, phonograph records, and many other things.

---

a bat, ā cake, ä father, är car, ãr dare; e hen, ē me, ėr term; i bib, ī kite, ir clear; o top, ō rope, ô saw, oi coin, ôr fork, ou out; u sun, ů book, ü moon, ū cute; ə about, taken

# W

**Wam·pa·no·ag** (wam′ pə nō′ äg′) *n. pl.,* **Wam·pa·no·ag** or **Wam·pa·no·ags.** a tribe of North American Indians that once lived in Rhode Island and Massachusetts.

**wan·dered** (won′ dərd) *v.* went or moved about without any particular plan; roamed.

**war·bling** (wôr′ bling) *v.* singing with quivers or trills, as a bird.

**war·ri·or** (wôr′ ē ər, wor′ ē ər) *n.* a person who fights or is experienced in fighting battles.

**Wash·ing·ton, George** (wô′ shing tən, wosh′ ing tən, jôrj′) 1732–1799, general in the American Revolution, and the first president of the United States, from 1789 to 1797.

**Wash·ing·ton, Mar·tha** (wô′ shing tən, wosh′ ing tən, mär′ thə) 1731–1802, the wife of George Washington.

**wast·ing** (wāst′ ing) *v.* using or spending in a careless or useless way.

**wealth** (welth) *n.* a great amount of money or valuable things; riches.

**wear** (wãr) *v.* to carry or have on the body.

**wea·ri·ly** (wir′ ə lē) *adv.* in a tired manner.

**whin·ing** (hwīn′ ing) *v.* crying in a complaining way.

**whin·nied** (hwin′ ēd) *v.* neighed, especially in a low, gentle manner.

**whit·tling** (hwit′ ling) *v.* cutting small bits or pieces from wood, soap, or the like with a knife.

**wil·der·ness** (wil′ dər nis) *n. pl.,* **wil·der·ness·es.** a place where no people live. In a wilderness there may be dense forests and many wild animals.

**wind·mill** (wind′ mil′) *n.* a machine that uses the power of the wind to turn large vanes at the top. Windmills are usually used to pump water or grind grain.

**wolf** (wulf) *n. pl.,* **wolves.** a wild animal that looks like a dog. Wolves have gray fur, a pointed muzzle, and a bushy tail. They live in cold, northern areas.

# Y

**yawned** (yônd) *v.* opened the mouth wide and took a deep breath.

**yoke** (yōk) *n.* a wooden frame used to join together two work animals.

# word work

This part of *Adventuring* is a review of letters and the sounds they stand for. Looking carefully at these letters will help you know how to say and read many new words.

## Lessons

# 1 Initial Consonants

Letters stand for sounds at the beginning of words.

___any ___onkeys ___ay ___ake ___ischief.

The sentence above does not make sense without the letters that stand for the beginning sounds. What one letter could you use to finish each word?

Number your paper from 1 to 9. Write the sentences below. Fill in the missing letters. Choose the letters from those in the box. Be sure the words make sense in the sentence.

| t d g b l w m c k |
| --- |

1. On ___ednesday ___endy and I ___ent for a ___alk.
2. We had ___ecided to hike the whole ___ay.
3. We packed ___ots of food for ___unch.
4. We ___ept finding things in the ___itchen.
5. Into our bags went ___any things to ___unch.
6. We also took along ___askets for ___erries.
7. We went ___ogether ___oward the ___op of a hill.
8. We hadn't ___one far before we began ___iggling.
9. We ___ouldn't ___arry all that stuff!

354

# 2 Final Consonants

Letters stand for sounds at the end of words.

| | | | | |
|---|---|---|---|---|
| ra**n** | robo**t** | instea**d** | wi**g** | chea**p** |

Some ending sounds can be spelled more than one way. Listen for the ending sounds:

| | | |
|---|---|---|
| cler**k**/blo**ck** | gue**ss**/bu**s** | foo**l**/sma**ll** |

Number your paper from 1 to 11. Each sentence below is missing one word. Notice the sound at the end of the underlined word in each sentence. Then find a word in one of the boxes above that ends with that same sound. Write both words on your paper.

1. I wanted to <u>get</u> a _____.
2. I took <u>ten</u> dollars and _____ to the corner.
3. I went <u>across</u> town on a _____.
4. I had to <u>walk</u> one _____ to the shop.
5. Inside was a <u>big</u> robot wearing a _____.
6. It had the <u>look</u> of a sales _____.
7. "Does this <u>shop</u> have any _____ robots?"
8. "Well, a _____ one is a hundred dollars."
9. I began to <u>feel</u> like a _____.
10. "<u>This</u> is not the store for me, I _____."
11. "I've <u>decided</u> to build one, _____," I said.

# 3 Short Vowels and Graphemic Bases

Read each word in the box below. Look at the underlined letter that spells each short vowel sound.

| a | e | i | o | u |
|---|---|---|---|---|
| f<u>a</u>n | n<u>e</u>t | sw<u>i</u>m | st<u>o</u>p | h<u>u</u>m |

**A.** Number your paper from 1 to 5. Read each sentence. Think of one vowel that will fit *all* of the blanks in the sentence. Then write the sentence on your paper.

1. The p___ppy had f___n outside in the m___d.
2. Wh___n B___n saw it, he wouldn't l___t it in.
3. He qu___ckly f___lled a tub w___th water.
4. He g___t a b___x of soap and a l___t of towels.
5. Soon th___t dog looked like a s___d, wet r___g!

**B.** Number your paper from 1 to 5. Write the words below. Next to each word, write a word from the box that rhymes.

1. bread     2. plan     3. sock     4. fit     5. stuck

| flock | mad | stick | red | duck |
|-------|-----|-------|-----|------|
| ten | clip | man | hit | sat |

# 4 Initial Consonant Clusters

The sounds of some letters blend together.
These letters are called consonant clusters.
Read this riddle:

What is <u>true</u> of <u>flower</u>, but not of tower?
It's something in the word <u>glue</u>.
You'll find it in words like <u>cross</u>,
    <u>grand</u>, <u>front</u>, and <u>blue</u>.
Do you have a <u>clue</u>?

The two letters at the beginning of each underlined word blend together. They are consonant clusters.

Number your paper from 1 to 8. Read each word clue below. Write your answer. Use one of the consonant clusters in the box to finish each word.

| cl | gl | fl | bl | cr | tr | gr | fr |
| --- | --- | --- | --- | --- | --- | --- | --- |

1. You do this when you're sad. ___y
2. You're always stepping on me! ___oor
3. I'll tell you the time. ___ock
4. Use me to build things. ___ocks
5. To get me, mix black and white. ___ay
6. Trains run on me. ___ack
7. You can wear me on your hand. ___ove
8. I'm someone you like. ___iend

# 5 Initial Consonant Clusters

Many consonant clusters begin with *s*. Look for consonant clusters as you read the story below.

As a little kid, I often rode a scooter. Then I decided to try a skateboard. I could just imagine myself swooping swiftly down a hill and sliding to a stop! But the day I first tried it, there were butterflies in my stomach. I was scared to death. I put on my sneakers and sweater, tied my scarf, and snapped my jacket. Then I carefully stepped onto the board and pushed off. I began to pick up speed. I smiled. Everything was going smoothly until suddenly I was on the ground. As I looked up, the sky seemed to be spinning. I had skinned my knee, too, but I wasn't sniffling. "This is the sport for me!" I thought, smiling.

**A.** Number your paper from 1 to 7. Write the consonant clusters below. Next to each, write the three words from the story that begin with the cluster.

| | | | |
|---|---|---|---|
| **1.** st | **2.** sn | **3.** sp | **4.** sc |
| **5.** sm | **6.** sw | **7.** sk | |

**B.** Write the two consonant clusters that stand for the same sound.

# 6 Final Consonant Clusters

Consonant clusters can come at the beginning or at the end of words.

Read the words below. Look at the underlined consonant clusters.

soft  last  think

plant  sold  stamp

Some important ending consonant clusters are listed in the box below.

| ft | st | nk | nt | ld | mp |

Number your paper from 1 to 6. Copy the sentences below. Fill in the blanks using consonant clusters from the box. Use the same consonant cluster for both of the blanks in each sentence.

1. Did I forget to tha___ you for the piggy ba___?
2. Can you ju___ over that stu___?
3. I ju___ bought my fir___ yo-yo!
4. Grandma le___ a gi___ for me on the table.
5. There are many wi___ flowers in that fie___.
6. The gia___ was very impatie___.

# 7 Long Vowels and Graphemic Bases

The words below show two ways to spell the long *a* vowel sound. Read the words. Look at the underlined letters.

c<u>a</u>ne        drivew<u>ay</u>

Now read the two words below. Look at the underlined letters. They show two ways to spell the long *i* vowel sound.

tr<u>i</u>be        fl<u>igh</u>t

Number your paper from 1 to 12. Read each set of words. Write the word that has a long *a* or long *i* vowel sound.

| | | | |
|---|---|---|---|
| **1.** quit | **2.** same | **3.** tickets | **4.** plan |
| quick | saucers | tight | plate |
| quite | saw | trick | park |
| **5.** spine | **6.** crab | **7.** mice | **8.** slipped |
| spill | crash | mint | slide |
| spin | crane | middle | slick |
| **9.** subway | **10.** grass | **11.** master | **12.** pick |
| sandwich | grade | mistake | pill |
| scratches | grant | monkey | pipe |

# 8 Long Vowels and Graphemic Bases

Read the two words below. The long *o* vowel sound can be spelled in these two ways.

br<u>o</u>ke      c<u>oa</u>t

Now read the word below. The underlined letters spell the long *u* vowel sound.

h<u>u</u>g<u>e</u>

Number your paper from 1 to 10. Read each sentence and the words that follow it. Write the sentence using the word that has a long *o* or a long *u* vowel sound.

1. Sam had a _____ called *Sunny.*    duck    boat
2. She was tied up with a _____.    knot    rope
3. One day there was a _____.    cyclone    rain
4. The tie _____.    broke    burst
5. Away *Sunny* _____.    bobbed    floated
6. Later, Sam was _____.    confused    puzzled
7. He searched until he found her washed up near a big _____.    stone    rock
8. There was a _____ in her side.    cut    hole
9. It took three people to _____ *Sunny.*    rescue    pull
10. Then it took two _____ days to fix her.    long    whole

# 9 Long Vowels and Graphemic Bases

Read the words below. Look at the underlined letters. The long e sound can be spelled in these two ways.

d<u>ee</u>p          h<u>e</u>

Number your paper from 1 to 12. Read the sentence below. Find the word with the long e vowel sound. Write the long e words on your paper. Underline the letter or letters that stand for this sound.

1. It was Mom who got me interested in birds.
2. She makes sure they visit our yard.
3. Now I help put seeds outside our windows, too.
4. Feeding the birds helps us learn about them.
5. Once we took a trip to a town far away.
6. Mom hoped to see a special bird there.
7. It lives in a big nest on top of a steeple.
8. Mom and I waited in the street, looking up.
9. All of a sudden, the stork came sweeping down.
10. It was by far the biggest bird I've ever seen!
11. The sight of it gave us a wonderful feeling.
12. How I wished I could be soaring through the sky on its back!

# 10 Initial Consonant Digraphs

Two or three letters may stand for one sound. Say the words below. Look at the underlined letters. Listen for the one sound the two letters make.

<u>sh</u>ift     <u>th</u>irty     <u>wh</u>isper     <u>ch</u>ase

Number your paper from 1 to 12. Use the underlined letters above to make a word for each sentence. Write the word on your paper. Be sure it makes sense in the sentence.

1. The wind ___istled that cold winter night.
2. Far away a horse ___innied.
3. It had yet to find ___elter from the storm.
4. The ___eep stayed close to each other for warmth.
5. They were lucky to be in a small ___ed.
6. Inside the house, a man sat ___ittling.
7. He was ___ankful to be near a warm fire.
8. A big pot of ___ili was cooking on the stove.
9. "There's nothing like a nice, warm supper," he ___ought.
10. "It will help to ___ase away the cold."
11. He filled a bowl and soon was ___ewing happily.
12. "I ___ink food tastes best this time of year," he said.

363

# 11  Final Consonant Digraphs

Read the following words. Notice how the two or three underlined letters make one sound.

su<u>ch</u>     bru<u>sh</u>     wor<u>th</u>     stro<u>ng</u>     pi<u>tch</u>

Read the story below. Look at the end of each underlined word.

Once there lived a <u>king</u> of great <u>strength</u> and <u>wealth</u>. Yet he was not happy. He told his servants to find him things to make him happy, but <u>each</u> came back <u>saying</u>, "<u>Nothing</u> in the world can <u>match</u> the wonderful things you have already." Now in that land there lived a poor man <u>with</u> a <u>patch</u> over one eye and a <u>crutch</u> to help him walk. Although he had little, he was always happy. When the king heard of this, he asked the man to <u>teach</u> him his secret. "I never <u>push</u>," the man replied, "and I never <u>rush</u>. Most of all, I never <u>wish</u> for too <u>much</u>." Then he smiled and was gone.

Number your paper from 1 to 5. Write each word below. Next to each word, write three words from the story that end with the same sound and are spelled the same way.

**1.** sandwich   **2.** watch   **3.** trash   **4.** ring   **5.** path

# 12 Syllable Generalizations

Some words can be divided into parts called syllables. To divide a word into syllables, first listen for the vowel sounds. Every syllable must have a sounded vowel.

Read these words: *feet, young, love.* How many vowel sounds do you hear in each word? How many syllables are in each word?

Now read these words: *harbor, sudden, canvas.* Each of these words has two sounded vowels. Each has two syllables.

Number your paper from 1 to 8. Say each word below to yourself. Write **1** if the word has one syllable. Write **2** if the word has two syllables.

**1.** cell          **2.** council          **3.** daily          **4.** birch
**5.** curtain          **6.** wealth          **7.** control          **8.** nation

---

When two consonants stand between two vowels, the word is usually divided between the consonants.

---

har bor          sud den          can vas

Number your paper from 1 to 8. Write each word leaving a space between the syllables.

**1.** signal          **2.** cabbage          **3.** compete          **4.** also
**5.** subway          **6.** canyon          **7.** musket          **8.** shelter

# 13 Schwa Vowel Sound

The schwa is a special vowel sound. It can be spelled with *a, e, i, o,* or *u.*

Read the words below. The underlined letters stand for the schwa sound.

anim<u>a</u>l    kitch<u>e</u>n    counc<u>i</u>l    pil<u>o</u>t    circ<u>u</u>s

The schwa vowel sound can also be at the beginning of words, as in <u>a</u>bout and <u>u</u>pon.

Number your paper from 1 to 10. Write each underlined word below. Underline the vowel that stands for the schwa vowel sound.

1. It was a <u>beautiful</u> spring day.
2. Mrs. Parker finished her <u>breakfast</u> quickly.
3. She got her paints and brushes and a <u>canvas</u>.
4. She put on her old <u>apron</u>.
5. She had noticed a <u>crocus</u> blooming.
6. A painting of the first flower of spring would make a good birthday <u>present</u> for her friend.
7. But, <u>alas</u>, when she got outside, the flower was gone!
8. Then she saw the <u>reason</u>.
9. A <u>quiet</u> little rabbit was happily munching.
10. The artist got out her <u>pencil</u> and paper and drew a picture of the rabbit, instead!

# 14 Diphthongs

Some vowel combinations make the same sound spelled with different letters.

clown/mouse        toy/poison

**A.** Write the words *clown* and *toy* at the top of your paper. Under each word, write the six words from the list below that have the same vowel sound.

boys   noun  mountain  turmoil  allowed  embroidery
moist  owls  shower    royal    destroy  mouthful

**B.** Number your paper from 1 to 9. Use letters from those in the box to make a word or words for each sentence. Write the words.

| oi | oy | ou | ow |
|----|----|----|----|

1. The airport was very n___sy.
2. I went to the cr___ded waiting room.
3. Finally I f___nd a seat.
4. Then I heard a v___ce from a l___dspeaker.
5. But what had it ann___nced?
6. I began to feel ann___ed and I fr___ned.
7. I began to wonder if I would enj___ my trip.
8. Then I realized h___ silly I was.
9. Such little problems wouldn't sp___l my fun.

## 15 *r*-controlled Vowels

The letter *r* changes the sound of the vowel it follows.

Look at each word pair below. Are the vowel sounds the same in—

jam and jar?
jet and jerk?
cut and curl?
won and work?
gift and girl?

**A.** Number your paper from 1 to 4. From each list write the two words that *rhyme.*

| **1.** shed | **2.** mist | **3.** spur | **4.** funny |
|---|---|---|---|
| herd | first | put | pony |
| nod | worst | her | worry |
| word | lost | let | hurry |

**B.** Number your paper from 1 to 4. From each list write the two words in which *r* changes the vowel sound.

| **1.** bargain | **2.** programs | **3.** sprawled | **4.** modern |
|---|---|---|---|
| fruit | article | circle | write |
| grand | mermaid | brilliant | scars |
| artist | through | purse | rawhide |